The BACH FLOWERS TODAY

Mark Wells

Disclaimer

The information and advice contained in this book is not intended to replace the services of a qualified health professional. Consult your health physician for advice. Use of the information contained herein is beyond the control of authors and publisher, who are not responsible for any problems arising from its application.

Mark Wells
P.O. Box 79
Kew East VIC 3102
Australia

www.wellsnaturopathy.com.au

© Mark Wells January 1993
© Mark Wells October 2013

All rights reserved. No part of this publication may be reproduced, stored in a retrieval system or transmitted in any form by any means without the prior permission of the copyright owner.

First Printing 1993 by Jenkin Buxton Printers Pty Ltd
Revised Edition 2013 by Mark Wells

Editing Clean Text

Cover Design & Interior Layout
By
Ian Hayward

Printed in Australia
By
Mark Wells

ISBN 0 646 15934 8

THANK YOU

My children, Samantha and Dean

Ian Hayward for his creative IT

Angela Rockel for her impeccably Clean Text

And of course Dr Edward Bach and his works for their help and positive influence on me (and the world).

Contents

Page No.

How to use this book	1
About the Bach Flowers	5
Agrimony	11
Aspen	13
Beech	15
Centaury	17
Cerato	19
Cherry Plum	21
Chestnut Bud	23
Chicory	25
Clematis	27
Crab Apple	29
Elm	31
Gentian	35
Gorse	37
Heather	39
Holly	41
Honeysuckle	43
Hornbeam	45
Impatiens	47
Larch	51

Contents

Page No.

Mimulus..55
Mustard..57
Oak..59
Olive..61
Pine...63
Red Chestnut..65
Rock Rose...67
Rock Water...69
Scleranthus..71
Star of Bethlehem.................................73
Sweet Chestnut.....................................75
Vervain..77
Vine...79
Walnut...81
Water Violet..83
White Chestnut.....................................85
Wild Oat..87
Wild Rose..89
Willow...91
Rescue Remedy....................................93
Index...95

How To Use This Book

The purpose of this book is to give everyone an opportunity to experience the benefits of using the Bach Flowers. I believe these remedies can help bring about profound improvements to quality of life.

ABOUT THE BACH FLOWERS

The section is intended both as an introduction for the novice and as clarification for more experienced users of Bach Flower remedies. Basic questions about the remedies are answered, drawing primarily on my own many years' experience as a practitioner, and also on experience and feedback gained from participants in the courses I teach, from colleagues and fellow-writers in the field, including, naturally, Dr Bach's own extensive writings.

BACH FLOWERS: AGRIMONY — WILLOW, AND RESCUE REMEDY:

Each entry is listed under its common and botanical names. This is followed by a general description of the type of person who responds best to the remedy under discussion (see page 6 'selective sensitivity'). This is a condensed overview of characteristic attitudes and behaviours – an archetypal picture, derived from the many people who have responded favourably to each particular Bach Flower remedy in my own practice and that of others. If the core issues described in relation to a remedy correspond to what is happening for you NOW, taking this remedy will give you a great opportunity to feel better and to make profound, positive changes in your life. The remedy picture does not need to match in every detail.

Internal subheadings for individual remedies have been arranged to enable quick and accurate reference, as follows:

- **Possible physical imbalances:** To date, this aspect of the negative states addressed by the Bach Flower remedies has not been extensively explored. I have included it because of my personal passion to discover the mental and emotional preconditions that contribute to physical illness. I believe we cannot be cured without reference to these subtle aspects of our beings. I believe also that while the Bach Flower remedies are by no means the only way to influence mental and emotional states, they are certainly one way that is safe and gentle.

Under this subheading are descriptions of:

a) General and specific *physical problems encountered most commonly in those who responded well to the remedy* under discussion, as I have encountered them in practice.

b) What I have learned from experience about body systems most likely to be affected in certain personality types according to esoteric law, especially in relation to the chakras.

Over the years, the experience gained in the first area has validated the insights of the second. These connections will continue to be made as we all become more enlightened about the subtle links between mind and body.

Never choose a Bach Flower remedy on physical symptoms alone, although symptoms may be used to confirm a choice based on personality type. Physical manifestations of a mental and emotional state are very likely to improve following a positive change of mind.

- **Classical uses:** This section describes a group of specific situations in which the remedy may be useful. Do not choose a Bach Flower remedy on the indication of one of these situations alone. They are intended as key points in an overview of the remedy – quick references to steer you towards an appropriate choice or towards a better understanding of the full remedy picture.

- **Complementary Bach Flowers:** Remedies listed in this section are those I have often found to be appropriate for use in conjunction with the Bach Flower being discussed. They may complement it by covering a different facet of the pattern, or their closely related qualities may reinforce its action.

Often the overlap and/or differences creates a synergistic effect. The components enhance one another in the way that those of Rescue Remedy do.

- **Supportive measures:** This section explores ways of enhancing and supporting the healing action of the Bach Flower remedies. By developing certain life skills and engaging in appropriate activities and therapeutic techniques, we can maximise our response to the remedies. I have included suggestions for making the most of opportunities to practise externally the positive internal changes that are happening. I also discuss possibilities for self-nurture during periods of vulnerability that sometimes arise when change is occurring at a deep level.

About the Bach Flower remedies

The Bach Flowers are a set of thirty-eight healing remedies. They come in a bottled liquid form and are taken orally a few drops at a time. They are completely naturally derived and are made directly from specially selected flowers, picked at the time in their blooming that will give them the greatest healing power.

In the early 1930s Dr Edward Bach, a successful and prominent UK physician, became aware that for most of his patients, it was emotional and mental factors that predisposed them to physical ailments. A very compassionate man, he wished to help his patients in a more profound way than seemed possible using the treatments available to him at the time. Accordingly, he developed a healing system that could positively influence people on the subtle levels at which illnesses arise. Over a number of years he put his sensitivity and scientific training into action to collaborate with nature, and so develop his world-renowned thirty-eight remedies.

WHAT CAN THEY DO?

The Bach Flower remedies act as a catalyst for positive inner transformation. They can, through raising self-awareness, assist us to transform our most negative states: fear, uncertainty, loneliness, oversensitivity to outside influences and despondency, into the corresponding positive states: courage, clarity, independence and peace of mind. They can help develop self-esteem, assertiveness, self-reliance and self-discipline, and above all, spontaneity and warmth in relationships.

Working with the Bach Flowers is like conspiring with nature to gain emotional security, health and well-being.

Like blossoming flowers, we can open up to a deeper understanding and appreciation of ourselves, others and our world.

HOW DO THEY WORK?

The best way to understand how the Bach Flowers work is to use them yourself. This is a subjective experience — there are as many descriptions of how they work as there are people using them, and that's a lot!

- **Selective sensitivity response:** This idea is my contribution to the body of Bach Flower experience. It can be summarised in the following way. The inherent life force unique to each Bach Flower is captured and preserved in liquid form. This liquid acts as the medium between plant and person. *If someone has strong similarities to the personality profile of a particular remedy, they will be sensitive to it. This means that the distinctive life-force pattern of the remedy will act as a blueprint for change on the emotional level. The selective sensitivity response can be compared to the way different people respond favourably to hearing different music, to seeing different paintings, or even to wearing different clothes. Everyone has a unique and absolutely valid response.*

By taking Bach Flowers one develops a raised awareness, not only of the aspects of self that are interfering with one's quality of life, but also of one's potential for changing those difficult aspects for the better. Of course we are free to choose what we do with this awareness; no change is forced upon us by the remedies. We are simply offered a view of our full potential.

HOW ARE THEY MADE?

The most common method of flower essence preparation is called the Sun Method, as devised by Dr Bach. Briefly, this involves sprinkling recently-picked blooms over the surface of pure spring water in a crystal bowl. The bowl is left out in full sunlight for a specified period of time, after which the flowers are removed from the bowl. The remaining sun-potentised liquid is combined with an equal amount of brandy — a natural preservative. This liquid is often referred to as the Mother Tincture. The Stock Bottle is prepared by putting two drops of Mother Tincture in a small bottle filled with pure brandy. Stock liquid may be used medicinally by taking two drops on the tongue four times a day. Single or combined remedies are also made from Stock — four drops to a 25ml bottle, for example, containing spring water and approximately one third brandy or vodka (or vegetable glycerin or apple cider vinegar) to act as a preservative. This is called dosage strength, to be taken four drops at a time, four times daily.

Dr Bach also used a Boiling Method to prepare some remedies. It is a similar process to the Sun Method, except that instead of being exposed to the sun, the plant material is boiled.

HOW DO I TAKE THEM — HOW OFTEN AND WHEN?

Bach Flower remedies are taken orally, either directly onto the tongue via a glass dropper, or in a small amount of water which is sipped slowly. As previously mentioned, the ideal frequency of dose is four times daily. In acute cases, such as after an accident or other trauma, the remedies may be taken more frequently (even as often as every 5 minutes for half an hour or so).

We are most susceptible to the healing influence of Bach Flowers at bedtime and on arising – at these times we are usually most relaxed, and so most receptive. Also, during sleep we process much of the day's stress, and receive insights from the unconscious. The two other doses should be taken as evenly apart across the day as possible — just before lunch and just before the evening meal are good times.

NB: Other times that are absolutely ideal for taking the remedies are: while having a bath (they may also be put in the bathwater); after meditation and relaxation practices; during therapy, or any other time you feel particularly relaxed, secure and receptive.

ARE THE BACH FLOWER REMEDIES SAFE?
DO THEY PRODUCE ANY SIDE EFFECTS?

They are completely safe. *There is NO possibility of a toxic effect,* because the physical amount of plant substance in the remedy is so minute. Infants, children, the elderly and even pets respond positively to well-chosen Bach Flower remedies with *absolutely no side effects.* In a very few cases there may be a heightened awareness of a particular feeling, for example, while grieving. One may for a short time be more aware of feelings of sadness, in the process of letting go of grief. This is a natural and positive experience, easily managed by adjusting frequency of dose to suit individual needs. Most people accept the process and quickly move on to a more peaceful state of mind.

WHO CAN PRESCRIBE THEM?

Anyone can prescribe the Bach Flower remedies. Dr Bach worked to develop a totally safe and effective natural healing system that was easy to understand and apply. He wanted it to be easily accessible to all. Naturally, the more familiar one becomes with the remedies through personal experience, reading, courses etc., the more effective and proficient one becomes at prescribing for oneself and others. Professional health practitioners have been prescribing the Bach Flowers for over seventy years. More recently, the remedies have become widely used by lay-people also, prescribing for themselves, family, friends and even pets. *Bach Flowers have an in-built safety mechanism. If you choose a remedy that is not appropriate, the worst effect it can have is absolutely NO effect.*

HOW LONG DO I NEED TO TAKE THEM?

This depends on the nature of the problem. A long-term problem – one that first manifested in early childhood for example, is unlikely to resolve itself overnight. A remedy may be taken for some months, and then later for some months again as different aspects of the problem gradually resolve, and new insights are gained. On the other hand, a more recent emotional trauma may require only a few doses of the appropriate remedy to give significant relief. The length of time depends entirely on the nature of the issue being addressed. After having a good response to a remedy, there may be no need to take it again for years — there is no need to continue after the problem is resolved.

HOW MANY REMEDIES CAN I TAKE AT ONE TIME?

Dr Bach's researches and my own experience in private practice for many years indicate that the ideal number of remedies to take at one time is between one and four. It appears that taking more than four remedies simultaneously makes them less effective. This may be because it is too overwhelming to deal with so many personal issues at one time, hence the temptation to stop, or just 'forget' to take the remedy. Sometimes too many remedies have a diluting effect on each other, and the overall result is a more superficial one. (Rescue Remedy is a separate case, and will be considered elsewhere in the book.)

HOW DO I SELF-PRESCRIBE?

The key to choosing the most appropriate remedy for yourself lies in what you feel at this moment. Matching how you feel now with the descriptions of Bach Flower emotional states will direct you to the remedy most beneficial to you. Often it is easy to relate a remedy to your past experience, *but I stress the importance of choosing according to present feelings, rather than from an intellectual analysis of your personal life-history.*

HOW DO I PRESCRIBE FOR SOMEONE ELSE?

You prescribe for someone else in the same way that you would prescribe for yourself. You must ascertain his or her current feelings, attitudes and state of mind. From this information you can choose appropriate remedies for their use.

Agrimony
(Agrimonia eupatoria)

Positive state
integration of life's light and shade
– inner peace

Negative state
repression of sadness – inner torment
social 'mask'

Agrimony people in the negative state fear the consequences of exposing their true selves to others. We are not all comfortable with what we believe to be our darker side, and some of us go to great lengths to avoid uncovering it, hiding real feelings behind an easy-going, cheerful facade. We firmly believe that if we revealed our true feelings, it would provoke rejection and even contempt in others. We spend the whole day attempting to stay above it all, suppressing the inner pain and worry that haunts us. It is only at night, without the distractions of the day, that the pain emerges and demands our full attention. A restless, sleepless night usually follows, unless we have drunk to excess in an effort to dull the inner torment. If so, we may have a few hours of alcohol-induced sleep, only to wake in the morning with the gut in a knot and the mind in a vivid state of worry over issues left unaddressed.

Agrimony can help free us from self-imposed emotional bondage, so that we can be comfortable about expressing honestly what we feel and who we really are. We no longer have to hide behind being the life of the party, at every party. We don't have to pretend we are happy when we are not. A true feeling of cheerfulness comes very naturally to the Agrimony person when he or she can also give vent to other emotions. All aspects of the self are seen and accepted in a new light by one who is outwardly fully expressed, and therefore inwardly contented.

POSSIBLE PHYSICAL IMBALANCES

The body often expresses what the mind cannot. In this case the skin of the Agrimony person may express toxicity through acne and associated skin complaints — a physical manifestation of emotional toxicity. (If the remedy description fits, teenagers can often benefit.) Digestive disorders are common — a 'blocked gut' reaction to the world — with associated liver involvement. The digestive tract may be literally churning and knotting in the attempt to control inner reactions.

CLASSICAL USES

For disguised inner torment and worry; for insomnia from worry; for addictions and dependencies in the Agrimony type; for fear of intimacy and intense emotion; for escapism — into movies, travel, drugs etc.; for the withdrawn teenager; to help open up the heart to the world, and to give protection and support in the process.

COMPLEMENTARY BACH FLOWERS

Mimulus — when there is a strong fear of others' reaction to you.
Cherry Plum — when you fear that you may do something desperate if the mental torture and worry does not cease.
Pine — when there is a feeling of guilt about living a lie.
Crab Apple — when there is self-disgust about the parts of you that are hidden from the world.

SUPPORTIVE MEASURES

- Study the Jungian concept of the Shadow. Gently explore self-analysis, but always in the presence of someone you trust — perhaps someone with training in the area who can listen and give feedback about your discoveries.

- Maintain a healthy diet and lifestyle. Choose exercise and activities that are vigorous and outgoing rather than passive.

- Until you are really confident of the changes in yourself, avoid social situations where you feel under pressure to perform in some expected way. Look for situations where you are comfortable enough to behave in a manner that feels more like the real you.

Aspen
(Populus tremula)

Positive state
security and inner protection

Negative state
nameless dread

Aspen people feel as though they have been born with a psychic 'thin skin'. There is an ever-present feeling of vulnerability, as if they have been placed on this earth without any real protection. The world for them is like one huge haunted house — they feel a constant sense of impending danger that has no rational basis. Like the aspen tree whose leaves tremble in anticipation of a breath of wind even on the stillest day, they live in constant apprehension.

Aspen should be considered when everyday activities make us anxious and fearful. Waking up in the morning and contemplating the day, leaving the house for work, driving the car, greeting work-mates, coming home to an empty house — all these things may be filled with a sense of dread and apprehension. This remedy may also be appropriate for temporary, but nonetheless acute states of mind such as nightmares in either children or adults. Fearfulness resulting from the use of mind-altering drugs, or just from watching a scary movie, responds well to Aspen. Those days when we have an uneasy sense that something is going to happen — we know not what — are very characteristic of the negative Aspen state.

The remedy can help us feel as though we have developed a thicker skin, without losing the sensitivity of our nature. It helps us to comfortably bring our unconscious fears into the light of consciousness, so that they no longer act as obstacles to a full and enjoyable life.

POSSIBLE PHYSICAL IMBALANCES

People in the negative Aspen state experience all the body's fear-reactions — shaking, goose-bumps, even circulatory changes such as raised pulse-rate, palpitations etc. Always being in a fearful 'fight-or-flight' state means that adrenal and kidney complaints can develop through over-stimulation. Fear has its primary effect in these areas.

CLASSICAL USES

For fears of unknown origin; for repeated nightmares; for the nervous, 'shaky', oversensitive person; for fears arising from mind-altering experiences; for the reluctant psychic — and the 'psychic sponge'; to develop a more secure sense of personal boundaries.

COMPLEMENTARY BACH FLOWERS

Aspen combines well with other fear remedies such as **Cherry Plum**, **Mimulus** and especially **Rock Rose**, whose negative state is one of absolute terror.

SUPPORTIVE MEASURES

- Meditation techniques, and especially visualisation of symbolic white light, can be used to strengthen one's sense of inner protection. In this way one's reserves of nervous energy are not so easily depleted.

- Avoid mind-altering drugs — even caffeine, alcohol and sugar — and other experiences that leave you negatively impressed, such as scary films, hysterical social situations etc.

- Find or create your own special refuge — a meditation room or chapel-like room where you feel safe and secure. Go there in body or in spirit whenever you need to.

Beech
(Fagus sylvatica)

Positive state
not affected by others' differences

Negative state
rigid intolerance

Beech people in the negative state are often slaves to their reactions to others who are different from them. Their intolerance of differing views, behaviours, beliefs and attitudes eats away at them until they are too exhausted to care. This is the only time they get any relief from their relentless over-concern about others.

In the Beech negative state we find ourselves screaming (just out of earshot) at the offender, or at someone on the television screen: 'Can't you see? How can you think like that?' or 'What's wrong with these people?' How easily the fragile sense of self, arising from a rigid and therefore brittle mind-set, can be shattered by surrounding influences!

Beech trees are actually weak and shallow-rooted, falling in storm winds if they are exposed by woodland clearance. In beech woods, other shrubs and trees are not tolerated – a dense canopy and thick layer of dropped beech leaves prevents their growth. However, mature, healthy beeches are refined and beautiful trees that have a lovely, balanced shape. As a remedy, Beech can help develop a protective buffer against feelings of invasion by different ways of being, allowing us to really appreciate, from a comfortable personal distance, the variety of styles that exist in the world. By developing better-defined personal boundaries, we are able to come to a better definition of our own truths. This makes us less judgemental of others – we no longer need to form our own protection racket! Our capacity is increased to accept and welcome the differences that make each of us unique. Variety is the spice of life.

POSSIBLE PHYSICAL IMBALANCES

Oversensitivity and over-reactivity can frequently manifest as over-reactions to the physical environment — food intolerances, hay fever and skin reactions. In the negative Beech state, energy is easily drawn in many directions, especially on a mental level, so that it is possible to become quite drained, both mentally and physically. Burn out and immune system depletion can occur.

CLASSICAL USES

For the irritability that goes with intolerance; for the judgemental perfectionist; for the refined/sensitive person easily affected by a physically or emotionally negative environment; for those who are easily 'sucked in' and provoked; to enable one to see others' positive aspects more clearly.

COMPLEMENTARY BACH FLOWERS

Walnut — when one is unduly influenced by the emotional demands of others.

Impatiens — when intolerance is accompanied by impatience.

Olive — when there is accompanying exhaustion.

SUPPORTIVE MEASURES

- Meditation and visualisation techniques are very useful in helping develop a sense of oneness and common ground, creating a positive balance between self and the world.

- Identifying and avoiding foods and other substances for which you have intolerances will mean quicker progress towards health and well-being. Beech can then help eliminate the predisposition to intolerance on the subtle, emotional level at which it arises.

- Regular cleansing diets are of great value because of the tendency to become easily 'toxic' on all levels.

- Study the Law of Harmlessness — form follows function, follows thought.

Centaury

(Centaurium erythraea)

Positive state
service as mutual exchange

Negative state
'doormat' mentality

We often respond too easily to the demands of others. It is possible to become a 'yes-person' through inability to recognise or acknowledge what we really want – it seems easier to respond in a knee-jerk fashion to someone else's requests. In the negative Centaury state, parents do it all for their children without giving them the opportunity to learn from their own mistakes. At work, becoming the person who always obliges, accommodating every workmate's demand, is a negative Centaury characteristic. In these situations, unhealthy relationships based on dependency develop. Further, the child or workmate may come to resent his or her dependence, feeling stifled and restricted in growth towards self-sufficiency.

In healthy relationships we are able to create enough space to allow room for our personal needs to be met. Centaury functions to allow contact with, and then recognition and acceptance of, our own innermost needs and desires. It helps us respond to our own needs as well as those of others. This is the true art of service in the world — to create a mutually beneficial exchange between people. The centaury plant can easily be overlooked and even walked on, but the flower once noticed can only be admired for its delicacy and beauty of form and colour. Centaury can help us to notice this beauty in ourselves and allow the needs and dreams of the inner child to remain in awareness. It is this child in us whose urgent needs and desires keep us in contact with the true joy and vitality of life.

POSSIBLE PHYSICAL IMBALANCES

Digestive complaints are common. All areas of the gut are vulnerable, being related to the Solar Plexus, where our true feeling-reaction to life resides. It is often only as a result of physical illness that people in the negative Centaury state will give themselves a reprieve from service to those dependent on them.

CLASSICAL USES

For the 'yes-person'; for those who allow themselves to be exploited by others; to help contact the inner child and its needs; to help understand what your own needs are and learn how to meet them yourself, rather than be dependent on others.

COMPLEMENTARY BACH FLOWERS

Walnut — to create space for positive change by giving protection from outside influences.

Scleranthus — when there is hesitancy in decision-making — 'Will I — won't I?'

Pine — when guilt stops you saying 'No', even though it is appropriate to do so.

SUPPORTIVE MEASURES

- Put aside an hour or two each day that is entirely for you, and under no circumstances give it over to someone else.

- Explore your past and current interests and enjoyments, and try to incorporate more of them in your life.

- When someone asks you to do something, pause and ask yourself, 'Will this help both of us?' Stop the knee-jerk yes-reaction and think about it!

- Try workshops and courses that contact and explore the world of the inner child.

Cerato
(Ceratostigma Willimottianum)

Positive state
contact with inner guidance

Negative state
search for external authority

For people in a negative Cerato state, self-doubt rocks the foundations of life. With no faith in the fundamental structure of their world-view, they constantly seek guidance from outer authorities to provide their lives with overall direction and form. The analogy of a child with a colouring-in book is useful — Cerato people are very good at colouring-in their lives to the last detail, but they desperately seek someone else to provide the outline. The final effect is never truly their own, and they feel as if they are only a proxy, filling in someone else's vision. Some element of self-doubt is constructive, as it leaves us open to change and growth, but an excess can leave us unable to recognise what change is appropriate for us. Stuck in destructive habits, we can become doctor-shoppers, always in search of advice we want to hear. Paradoxically, this apparent search for the new may simply be another form of sticking with the devil you know, seeking the one who will give permission to stay the same. We may even take what we know to be wrong advice because we are unable to hear the inner voice that says, 'This is right for you.' We do not trust our own judgement enough to recognise the right advice and direction even when it is in front of us.

Cerato helps release us from these restrictive habits, so that we are free to contact the wise self that is waiting to guide and direct our lives from within.

POSSIBLE PHYSICAL IMBALANCES

The Throat Centre is especially influenced by Cerato, so that in the negative state there is a strong possibility of recurring throat problems. Lymphatic congestion — a 'rubbish disposal' or discernment problem — can lead to immune system weakness and proneness to infection.

CLASSICAL USES

For self-doubt and negative self-judgement; for the chronic advice-seeker; for the doctor-shopper seeking the practitioner who will give them permission to stay the same; for the actor who has no identity outside his or her role; for those who ask for advice but never take it; to help create a life that reflects one's true, positive personality.

COMPLEMENTARY BACH FLOWERS

Elm — when one is overwhelmed by the huge number of possible responses to questions and difficulties.

Larch — when one has little confidence in one's ability to carry out life-tasks.

Gentian — when one has become very discouraged by past mistakes.

SUPPORTIVE MEASURES

- Take positions of responsibility — be head of a committee or captain of a team when you are asked to!
- Work in situations where you will be called upon for guidance you know you are competent to give. This will help restore your confidence in how much you have to offer others, and therefore yourself, in the way of guidance and direction. Learn about self-esteem and self-assertiveness.
- HAVE A GO!!

Cherry Plum
(Prunus cerasifera)

Positive state
trust and calm under stress

Negative state
pushed-too-far-feeling

We all endeavour to maintain control in our lives, taking practical steps to insure ourselves and our families against rough times that may threaten us. We put away money in the hope that we may keep our independence later in life. But however much we try, we cannot control all variables. Freedom from anxiety, then, depends largely on the degree to which we can trust the fate which contains these unknown factors. Fear of losing control – emotionally, financially or even mentally — inhibits experience and appreciation of life.

We may contract into a guarded existence, or, in particularly stressful or out-of-control times, we may fear that we will do the previously unthinkable. Things we thought were reserved for those far less fortunate than ourselves — murder, insanity, suicide — become vividly present possibilities, rising out of the Shadow to which they are normally relegated. Fortunately these mental images seldom become reality, but we go through hell thinking about them.

Cherry Plum helps release us from the obsession with control which can become all-pervasive, affecting our children, partners, extended family and even clients, suppressing our own spontaneity and that of those around us. This remedy helps give us faith in the unlimited resources that are available to us through the higher self, so that we can meet life poised and calm. Surrendering to inner guidance, we let go of the fear of death and dying, taking hold of life and living.

POSSIBLE PHYSICAL IMBALANCES

The condition of the stomach says a lot about our receptivity to life-experience — how we are surrendering to the moment. Accordingly, stomach problems are common for those in a negative Cherry Plum state. The nervous system can also be affected in its role as originator and controller of action in organs and tissues. Overstimulation is common, manifesting as nervous tension and muscle spasm.

CLASSICAL USES

For fears about doing something desperate; for fear of going crazy; for fears about what you might do if pushed too far; for fear and denial of the Shadow side; for the desperado; to help one trust every part of the self; to remain calm in difficult situations; to help get a grip on things.

COMPLEMENTARY BACH FLOWERS

Cherry Plum is an important ingredient in **Rescue Remedy**, enhancing the synergistic effect of the other remedies.

SUPPORTIVE MEASURES

- Study the Jungian concept of the Shadow — that part of the unconscious that holds everything we consciously choose not to do or be.

- Surrender control in some area of your life at least once a day – let someone else drive the car for a change! Take a back seat sometimes in other ways too.

- Try relaxation techniques that will teach you how to 'let go'.

- Take a few risks!

Chestnut Bud

(Aesculus hippocastanum)

Positive state
mistakes used as learning experiences

Negative state
failure to learn from mistakes

Think of Chestnut Bud for anybody continually falling back into old self-defeating habits – the child at school who makes the same mistakes over and over so that learning is impeded; the person in business who doesn't recognise a recurring problem and repeats the same errors of judgement; the person who repeatedly falls back into old addictive, self-destructive behaviours related to food, drugs, sleep patterns etc., without apparently gaining any insight; when history repeats itself.

Chestnut Bud helps make us aware of the warning signs that point to a recurrence of old destructive life-patterns. This raised awareness allows us better overview in our lives. We can contact both our inner wise teacher and the inner receptive student keen for guidance. The remedy can help maintain concentration, clarity and focus, allowing us to see our goals clearly, as well as the steps we need to take to reach them most easily. Most of all, Chestnut Bud helps us gain wisdom from life experiences.

POSSIBLE PHYSICAL IMBALANCES

Addictions, food sensitivities and intolerances are common, and in the negative Chestnut Bud state, these may be 'forgotten', and then indulgence is followed by the inevitable unpleasant consequences. Mental and physical fatigue may occur, related either to food intolerances, or to lack of motivation after repeated setbacks arising from failure to learn from experience.

CLASSICAL USES

For slow learners; for those repeating the same mistakes and not learning from experience; for the easily distracted person with a short concentration span; to get the best out of a learning experience; to find your inner guide.

COMPLEMENTARY BACH FLOWERS

Wild Oat — when one is unsure about general life-direction.
Crab Apple — when there is shame about mistakes.
Walnut — when one is easily knocked off course by inner or outer distractions and influences.

SUPPORTIVE MEASURES

- Become more accountable to yourself and others for your successes and failures in learning from experience – try making a daily chart of how well you're doing. It can show you how often you really ate chocolate this week, or how often you left the side gate open and let the dog out!

- Create learning-systems that will allow you to check your progress and observe behavior patterns.

- Look at methods as well as results.

Chicory

(Chicorium intybus)

Positive state
unconditional love
sense of own innate capacities

Negative state
conditional love
feelings of powerlessness

In the negative Chicory state we don't feel heard, and we lose trust in life's ability to meet our needs: 'No one cares about me!' When we feel like this we will go to great lengths to change the situation. Unfortunately, we often do it in unproductive ways, resorting to clingy and manipulative behaviour that only decreases our chances of getting what we want. We go for what we feel we deserve: 'Look at all I've done for you, and this is how you repay me!' The Chicory person has a lot of love to give but, too often, they don't feel appreciated for it.

If we don't have any trust that our needs will be met, our love is conditional – it becomes a sort of currency. We may also have a sense of missing out on our fair share when fear has stopped us responding to opportunities, and others have snapped them up. Sibling rivalry is an example of a negative Chicory pattern. With the arrival of a new baby, the older child desperately sets out to re-establish a sense of his or her place and importance in the family dynamic, constantly seeking the attention that has been 'taken away' by the baby: 'What about me?'

Chicory helps us communicate our needs effectively to those around us, and then helps us trust that those needs will be met. The signature of the plant tells all: flower buds form in clusters and open one after another in succession. Each one gets its time to blossom and be the radiant centre. Each gets what it needs. Chicory helps us trust life's abundance, and increases our ability to perceive its flow in our lives.

POSSIBLE PHYSICAL IMBALANCES

Chicory relates strongly to the Throat Centre. In the negative state there can be recurring throat complaints, especially in children. Any illness that arises when we feel powerless, or feel we are not receiving the attention and support we deserve, will respond well to Chicory.

CLASSICAL USES

For sibling rivalry; for the relentlessly attention-seeking child or adult; for habitual sulking; for manipulative behaviour; for feelings of powerlessness; for the sense of missing out; for the parent who wants to yell, 'What about me?'; to increase trust in universal abundance; to help receive and give unconditional love.

COMPLEMENTARY BACH FLOWERS

Willow — when there is resentment and a 'victim' mentality.

Vervain — when there is a desire to change others' behaviour towards you.

SUPPORTIVE MEASURES

- Learn effective communication and self-assertion so that you can use overt rather than covert ways to get what you want.
- Learn to criticise constructively, especially in relation to those close to you.
- Try to engage in activities that are self-nurturing (e.g. seeking company and interests that truly delight and nourish you), rather than those that are merely self-gratifying (e.g. consoling yourself with foods that actually make you sick, or overindulging in the pleasure of punishing those you feel have wronged you.)
- Learn to give and receive — presents, compliments — for no other reason than the joy of it.

Clematis
(Clematis vitalba)

Positive state
thoughts convert to action

Negative state
dreamy disorientation

People in the negative Clematis state have vivid and colourful thoughts which are seldom converted into action, because this mental world absorbs all their energy. They constantly escape back to the future from present responsibilities. It is easy for them to disappear into reading, watching movies, daydreaming or planning the future, at the expense of things and people of more immediate importance. Fantasy and daydreaming can be therapeutic in moderation, and are quite normal for children, but when they are constant in adult life they can prevent us from living our full potential. Like the clematis vine which has no means of supporting itself and so relies on other plants to hold it up, we can become dependent on others for support and structure in our lives if we never put any energy into day-to-day practicalities.

We all go through periods when we are easily distracted from a task we find mundane and unattractive, whether it is study for an exam or an unappealing project at work. Clematis can be very helpful during such temporary lapses in motivation, allowing us to convert thought into action.

Clematis helps give us the ability to be grounded enough so that our thoughts and ideas can take tangible form on earth. We begin to feel more comfortable in the present, and so become more productive and self-fulfilled. Optimism about life is renewed, and like the clematis plant itself, spreads fast.

POSSIBLE PHYSICAL IMBALANCES

Consider Clematis for the effects of concussion and shock (always seek medical advice as well), and for the after-effects of drug-abuse, jet lag, or anaesthetics, when disorientation results from a dislocation of the mind-body connection.

CLASSICAL USES

For perpetual daydreamers; for 'space cadets'; for mind-body dissociation; for inability to concentrate; for professional procrastinators; for those dependent on others for stability and system; to help make a commitment to life here and now.

COMPLEMENTARY BACH FLOWERS

Clematis makes a marvellous contribution to the effects of **Rescue Remedy**. In many cases where Clematis is appropriate, it may be taken as part of this combination.

It is useful to compare Clematis with Honeysuckle. While Clematis escapes from the present into the future, Honeysuckle escapes from the present into the past.

SUPPORTIVE MEASURES

- Engage in as many grounding activities as possible such as working with earth in some form — gardening, pottery etc., or bike-riding, bushwalking or any other physical exercise that will get the blood flowing and make you aware of your body, giving you a sense that it belongs to you.

- Put some routine in your life. It will help you develop a sense of responsibility and self-reliance, make you more accountable to yourself and others, and keep you mentally in tune with the present.

- Avoid spending too much time in meditation or other passive, primarily mental activities.

Crab Apple
(Malus sylvestris)

Positive state
sense of proportion about problems

Negative state
feels contaminated, even by minor imperfections

Crab Apple people in the negative state feel unclean in some way. Something feels not right. The blame for this may be focused primarily on one part of the body, or on one part of the personality. Obsessed by details of personal make-up, they lose perspective about what is really important in their lives and in the world.

In this state we get caught up in annoying minor details, becoming disconnected from the big picture. Or we may become pedantic, wasting time on trivia. The magic of full experience is lost. We may lose appreciation of the exquisite pleasure of love-making, focusing on body-parts and details of the physical act. A small skin blemish, a minute birthmark, or slight body odour may completely destroy our capacity to see our own beauty or that of others. Projecting all the shame and self-condemnation we have ever felt onto these minor idiosyncrasies, we highlight them out of all proportion.

Crab Apple is a cleanser on all levels. The pure white flower signifies this quality. It helps clear inherent and acquired taints so that we feel pure and free of spirit, more able to see the small problems of our earthly existence for what they really are — small!

POSSIBLE PHYSICAL IMBALANCES

Crab Apple will support any blood-cleansing diet or treatment where a sense of uncleanness is part of the presenting problem. The negative Crab Apple state will quite often include some 'toxic' or 'impure' symptoms such as acne or unpleasant body odour. It is also useful during brief periods of feeling yucky and toxic after overeating, and has been used for this sensation where it occurs with acute premenstrual symptoms with some success.

CLASSICAL USES

For those who feel contaminated in mind or body; for the sense of shame; for those obsessed about impure thoughts and unclean bodies; for over-concern about things that seem trivial to others; for those who think sex is dirty; for the prude; to allow us to see parts (especially private ones!) of the self in a broader context — to broaden our minds; to help us put our lives and problems in perspective.

COMPLEMENTARY BACH FLOWERS

Pine — when there is a sense of guilt and self-reproach about the cause of the 'impurity'.

Impatiens — when there is irritability and impatience over minor details.

Cherry Plum — when things experienced as sordid and unclean seem out of your control.

SUPPORTIVE MEASURES

- Cleansing and elimination diets will help. Moderate fasting on a regular basis is also useful, for example one day a week or fortnight eating only fruit or vegetables. As well as being cleansing, this allows you a broader approach to food in general, so that existing obsessions around food are modified, and new ones do not easily develop.

- Meditation and breathing techniques can be cleansing for both mind and body, as can aerobic exercise.

- If you're daring enough, try roughing it out in the bush — camping or bushwalking, to experience at first hand how the bugs, creepy-crawlies and dirt fit beautifully and naturally into the overall scheme of things.

Elm
(Ulmus procera)

Positive state
self-assured competence
sense of responsibility to self

Negative state
overwhelmed and anxious
over-committed to external projects

At those times when we feel overwhelmed by our life's tasks, and unable to complete them — when the responsibilities on which we have thrived till now seem the very things that will bring us down, we should consider Elm. Elm people accumulate responsibilities in order to provide a secure structure and a sense of worth in their lives. When this self-imposed load becomes too heavy to carry, their lives feel worthless and without direction.

You will find Elm people on every committee, at every working-bee — generally in charge, and above all, always available to others in need, like the Rock of Gibraltar. But even the Rock of Gibraltar can wear down and crack eventually! When commitments and obligations build beyond a tolerable level, a personal crisis can occur. Then we are forced to choose between the desire to take on more work in order to maintain a sense of worth, and the need for relief from overwhelming responsibility. In the end our own needs and those of people close to us make the choice clear.

Elm teaches us to acknowledge the responsibility we have to ourselves, and to recognise that meeting it is a God-given right. This can be difficult if our early interaction — or lack of it — with an authority figure such as Dad has left us with a sense of having to meet impossibly high standards. (Which we nevertheless spend the rest of our lives trying to achieve.)

The saying, 'A friend in need is a friend indeed' may well have been coined by an Elm person, wanting to describe his or her desire to be there for others in crisis. But that same person, feeling anxious and overwhelmed by the effort to extend limited energy too far, might later be heard to say, 'Only rogues give more than they've got to give.' Fortunately, Elm can help restore the self-assurance which is a trademark of its positive state. It does so by raising our awareness of our personal integrity, value, and right to a reasonable workload, relieving us of the constant urge to externally validate our existence. Ah, what a relief!

POSSIBLE PHYSICAL IMBALANCES

Headaches may be a feature of the negative Elm state — when the head is aching to follow the heart's needs. In general, Elm people tend to have strong physical constitutions, just like the elm tree, whose wood is prized in furniture-making for its qualities of strength and endurance. Because of this, illness often takes the form of moments of weakness in lives that are usually strong. For mere mortals, though, Elm is useful as a protection for the immune system during times of great responsibility or heavy workload.

CLASSICAL USES

For anxiety from overwhelming responsibility; for the weak moments in the lives of the strong (or the weaker moments in the lives of the less-strong); for the constant rescuer; for the constant approval-seeker; for those with something to prove — usually to Father; for those who deny their own needs; to give courage and poise when confronting life's tasks and ordeals; to enhance self-approval; to help nurture the inner child.

COMPLEMENTARY BACH FLOWERS

Hornbeam — when there is a feeling of weakness and lack of energy to cope with daily tasks.
Cherry Plum — when things (including yourself) feel totally out of control and you fear the outcome.
Willow — when you resent your responsibilities and feel a victim to your obligations.

For support before and during examinations or other situations in which you are called upon to 'perform', a good 'study mix' is Elm, White Chestnut, Clematis, Larch, Rock Rose.

SUPPORTIVE MEASURES

- Develop priorities that support your own needs and those of your loved ones.
- Look after yourself with regard to diet, exercise and lifestyle.
- Spend more time with your father, or do some therapeutic work on issues arising in your relationship to him.
- Put a higher value on yourself and your time.

Gentian

(Gentiana amarella)

Positive state
resilience in the face of setbacks

Negative state
depression of known origin
discouragement

Gentian helps when we have become discouraged and disheartened by setbacks at the level of our hopes and aspirations, particularly when we have put long hard work into achieving those aspirations. Failure to achieve a desired performance-level at a chosen sport, setbacks in promotion or business projects, the failure of a personal relationship that appeared at first to have great promise, or that ultimate trial, the loss of a loved one, can all leave us disillusioned, without the will to try again.

A big part of the problem is that our ideas about how life should be if we are to be happy are too set, and often not grounded in reality. When situations occur that do not fit neatly into our ideal scenario, we are disappointed and prone to give in.

Gentian helps us face life's challenges with courage, a light heart, and an uplifted viewpoint — an overview. It broadens our perspectives to allow us access to positive aspects of the situation. In this way we can tolerate the ups and downs of life with resilience, and an enduringly positive and purposeful attitude.

POSSIBLE PHYSICAL IMBALANCES

The Gentian depressive attitude can over time develop into a true depression that undermines physical health. There is no doubt that a permanently negative outlook eventually creates immune system dysfunction, sometimes taking the form of chronic or recurring viral infection.

CLASSICAL USES

For extreme discouragement after setbacks; for those who give up easily; for depression from a known cause; to help develop flexibility of outlook and a broader perspective; to help one to persevere; for those who want to believe but always find reasons not to; to help remain faithful to one's aspirations despite obstacles and setbacks.

COMPLEMENTARY BACH FLOWERS

Willow — when there is bitterness and resentment over disappointments.

Crab Apple — when you feel ashamed of what has happened (self-reproach and guilt respond to Pine).

Larch — when expectation of failure prevents you from trying again.

SUPPORTIVE MEASURES

- Explore the Buddhist philosophy which suggests that the road travelled is as important as the destination reached. 'Before enlightenment, chop wood and carry water, after enlightenment, chop wood and carry water.'

- A more philosophical and spiritually-based outlook will give you a context in which to view your problems.

- Above all, have another go – nothing ventured, nothing gained!

Gorse
(Ulex europaeus)

Positive state
sees 'light at the end of the tunnel'

Negative state
all is dark

Think of Gorse at those torrid times when bad news has come, a close friend has gone away, belongings have been lost through fire or theft, or when all is lost on the stock exchange.

Gorse helps rekindle the flame of life. When all seems lost and we are in despair, it can arouse a glimmer of hope, re-igniting the heart's desire to carry on, allowing us to see obstacles in a new light, as opportunities for growth and service.

The brilliant golden yellow of the flower reminds us of our potential to come shining through the darkest and bleakest times. Just as the gorse plant retains one or two flowers through the harshest winter, emerging in golden radiance in the spring, so we can emerge triumphant after soul-challenging times. This remedy helps conjure our deepest survival instincts to carry us out of the depths of despair into full life again. It guides us to the light at the end of the tunnel.

POSSIBLE PHYSICAL IMBALANCES

If the negative Gorse state persists too long, for some it can lead to eye and vision problems. A constantly dim view of the future can exacerbate existing short-sightedness, or lead to the development of conditions such as cataract and glaucoma. The body goes out in sympathy with mental attitudes and habits. A depressed immune system commonly follows a depressed state of mind.

CLASSICAL USES

For utter despair and a complete lack of faith in the future; for a 'clouded horizon'; for depression arising from the feeling of being in the twilight of life; for those who feel they have nothing to look forward to; to brighten up one's view of life; to restore faith and hope; to enable one to warmly embrace the future.

COMPLEMENTARY BACH FLOWERS

Wild Rose— when one feels resigned to the fact that life will remain miserable — 'Who cares anyway?'

SUPPORTIVE MEASURES

- Actively seek something you can put faith and energy into. Gorse will help clarify what this might be — a new creative outlet or interest, a new career path, or a revitalised philosophical or spiritual perspective.

- Avoid those who are doom and gloom merchants and seek out people who are optimistic and committed.

- Commit yourself to life!

Heather
(Calluna vulgaris)

Positive state
empathy with others

Negative state
self-obsessed neediness

Heather can help when our need to share thoughts and feelings becomes a compulsion for ourselves and a drain on others. In our desperate attempt to draw people closer to us in the search for comfort and recognition, we succeed only in repelling them. Our anxiety urgently seeks expression, and also validation by others — it doesn't matter who! The relationship exists solely in terms of whether or not they are willing to listen to us!

Self-obsession – about every detail of our health, our house, our finances, our safety when alone — has the effect of obscuring the overall picture. We can't see the wood for the trees, in our minds or in our lives. We have no ability to reflect in a meditative way, and our awareness has become confused and agitated — our thoughts disturb us and others like the cat among the pigeons.

Heather can help us to be more objective, so that the great sympathy and concern we are capable of towards ourselves can be transformed into an equal empathy for the plight of others. We can shift our absolutely inward-turning focus of concern and awareness outward to some degree, to include those around us. When the Heart Centre is balanced in this way, Heather people have a tremendous capacity for self-healing, through the healing of others.

POSSIBLE PHYSICAL IMBALANCES

Heather people in the negative state can be classic hypochondriacs. They become the health practitioner's nightmare, giving detailed accounts of their medical history and complaints that are nothing short of epics. Heather can help them gain a broader perspective on their state of health, allowing for a much more wholistic approach. General immunity improves when the thymus gland is better conditioned by a more balanced Heart Centre.

CLASSICAL USES

For the self-obsessed; for those who buttonhole others; for feelings of paranoia about being alone; for the hypochondriac; for those who are a drain on others in their company; to help us listen and really hear others; to help place our problems in a broader perspective.

COMPLEMENTARY BACH FLOWERS

Crab Apple — when we want our idiosyncrasies to be hidden – we are ashamed of them. (Heather, on the other hand, is equally obsessed by idiosyncrasies but wants to share them.)

Vervain — when we pester people in order to make them be like us.

Walnut — for protecting those who frequently spend time with someone in a negative Heather state.

SUPPORTIVE MEASURES

- Study wholistic medicine, or at least investigate its possibilities. This will help develop a broader perspective on health issues, and offer practical ways of improving quality of life.

- Work with people in need — your problems will appear in a different light.

- Practise meditation and other mind-body integrating disciplines.

Holly
(Ilex aquifolium)

Positive state
open-hearted love

Negative state
extreme negativity

The negative Holly state illustrates the concept that emotion is an energetic force that should be in a constant process of transformation. When it stagnates, problems arise. Bach Flowers are one very good way to get stagnant energy moving again, and Holly is a prime mover in this sense. It helps transform negative emotional states into their positive opposites, and in the process forms a protective barrier against outward negativity.

In the family we experience many love/hate relationships. They display how easily the nature of our emotions can undergo dramatic change, even in the space of a few minutes. Brothers and sisters may be happily playing together one minute and at each other's throats the next. A minute later, and the whole angry episode is completely forgotten and they are playing again. Healthy relationships allow emotion to remain in a state of flux. It is only when feelings are permanently negative that we have real problems. At these times Holly can help swing the pendulum away from envy, suspicion, hatred and desire for revenge, and towards feelings of love, compassion and trust.

The holly plant has always been a symbol of Christmas, a time we wish to dedicate to the celebration of our love and compassion for one another, but which also witnesses acts of extreme violence and hatred. Holly protects us against these kinds of darkness, and allows us to nurture the heart-energy that will allow our great potential for love to blossom in the world. We can fall in love with life again!

POSSIBLE PHYSICAL IMBALANCES

The chronic auto-immune disease and general immune system dysfunction that result from Heart Centre and thymus gland imbalance will benefit from the use of Holly, both now and even more certainly in the future.

CLASSICAL USES

For feelings of jealousy, envy, vengefulness and hatred; for those moments when, metaphorically speaking, you feel you could 'just kill'; for protection against the negative feelings of others; to open our hearts to love.

COMPLEMENTARY BACH FLOWERS

Walnut — when there is strong sensitivity to the negative emotions of others.

Cherry Plum — when negative feelings are so strong you are fearful of what you might do.

Crab Apple — when there are feelings of shame either during or after a 'negative Holly' episode.

SUPPORTIVE MEASURES

- Try to take time out by yourself and away from negative influences, for example in the greenness of the countryside. However you create it, you need space.

- Integrate more of the colours pink and green into your clothes and environment. They produce a feeling of secure space by their soothing and healing effect on the Heart Centre.

Honeysuckle

(Lonicera caprifolium)

Positive state
warmth and openness to present and future

Negative state
stuck in the past

In the negative Honeysuckle state, people have a belief that the past is much better than it actually was. The present could never live up to this glory, and so they never really live it. They always view both now and the future pessimistically, for fear that their distant ideal will fall off the pedestal on which they have placed it.

Honeysuckle can heal the heart, allowing it to gently unfold and receive life now, when it has previously been open only to the past.

Pining for the way we were earlier in a current relationship, or for how good it was in a past one; relentless heartache for the homeland when we make a new beginning elsewhere; inability to let go of the past we shared with a loved one lost long ago; emotional attachments that persist past their natural time; clinging to old beliefs and thought patterns that have become obsolete in our present circumstances — all these things can respond to the healing influence of Honeysuckle.

There are times in all our lives when we would like to withdraw from cold reality. Honeysuckle can help us experience the warmth that is available in the present, reawakening our affection for life.

POSSIBLE PHYSICAL IMBALANCES

In the negative Honeysuckle state, people often experience congestive symptoms in the head, which is working overtime to rule a heart that is pining for the past. Conditions such as sinus congestion, persistent nasal discharge and post-nasal drip — 'inner tears', and recurring head colds are common.

CLASSICAL USES

For acute nostalgia; for homesickness; for those whose pasts have become legends in their own minds; for those stuck in the good old days; to assist past-life and regression therapies; to help one become grounded in reality; to integrate heart and head; to greet life with an open heart.

COMPLEMENTARY BACH FLOWERS

Wild Rose — when one is resigned to the fact that life can never be as good as it was.

Willow — when one blames others for the decline in quality of life.

Compare Clematis with Chestnut Bud, which also shows lack of insight into reality.

SUPPORTIVE MEASURES

- Meditation and other practices that bring mental clarity will help centre the head and the heart in the present. Regression therapy may begin to resolve emotional attachments to the past, so that we can experience the present more fully.

- Grounding activities such as gardening and vigorous exercise will be of great benefit — anything that will get the red blood of life flowing through us.

- Accept the challenge of this reality. After all, that is why we chose to be here.

Hornbeam
(Carpinus betulus)

Positive state
freshness, strength and enthusiasm

Negative state
pacing oneself to get through the day

Hornbeam is for that Monday morning feeling all day, every day. When we wake and look towards the day ahead, what needs to be done seems insurmountable but unavoidable. Everything becomes just another chore, and though somehow we get through it all, we always fear that we will not. Much energy is wasted in concern over whether or not jobs will get done — we do them despite the fact that our minds are continually psyching us out, and diffusing the little energy we have. We feel we can't cope because we just don't have the strength.

Hornbeam can help get us out of this rut, whether we have fallen in it from sheer overwork as a first-time mother on call twenty-four hours a day, or as a workaholic suffering from burn out. The remedy lets us develop a fresh pattern with more healthy rhythms and new plans of action in work and play. It's a bit like approaching an old problem after a holiday or complete break. Hornbeam can help restore choice when we have become slaves to routine and habit because we just don't have the energy to change them, giving freshness and strength to our approach.

POSSIBLE PHYSICAL IMBALANCES

Hornbeam is one of the first Bach Flowers to think of (along with Olive) during rehabilitation after illness or after prolonged work that is very stressful. It should be considered whenever there is depression and depletion of energy associated with lingering illness. Where physical illness is not present, Hornbeam people usually soldier on despite chronic mental fatigue.

CLASSICAL USES

For those feeling they lack the strength to cope with everyday tasks; for those with a strong and rigid work ethic; for those who feel they need to pace themselves to get through the day; for the tired procrastinator; to help break out of a rut; to help bring vitality and freshness to a mundane existence; to help bring enthusiasm, joy and magic back into life; to help you follow your heart's desire.

COMPLEMENTARY BACH FLOWERS

Olive — when there is extreme exhaustion on both mental and physical levels.

Elm — when one feels overwhelmed and anxious at the thought of what needs to be done.

SUPPORTIVE MEASURES

- Take a break, or even better, take a holiday!
- 'All work and no play makes Jack a dull boy.' Try to incorporate more times of simple enjoyment in your life. Redefine your priorities.
- Take more interest in your health and lifestyle. Use natural dietary supplements, and ease into a pattern of regular exercise.

Impatiens
(Impatiens glandulifera)

Positive state
accepts differences in pace and style
process-oriented

Negative state
intolerant of others slowness
excessively goal-oriented

Impatiens people in the negative state have too much to do, and too little time to do it in. It seems that they arrive on earth like interplanetary tourists, desperately trying to pack as much sight-seeing as possible into their whirlwind tour. They feel different, alone and held back by the pace of others – these backward earthlings around them!

When we are in this state we are driven by a constant sense of urgency, with an insatiable desire for results. And although as individuals we are very capable of achieving those results, we inevitably suffer from overload and deadline delirium because of our inability to accept support from those around us. Our intolerance of, and impatience with the slow pace of others' work prevents us from developing good collaborative working relationships. 'Leave it alone! I'll do it. I'm the only one who can get the job done properly and on time!' is often our attitude. It quickly alienates us from others, supporting our self-fulfilling sense that we don't belong here.

In the positive state, Impatiens people have much to offer the world in the way of vision, inspiration, and the ability to be self-motivated in pursuit of goals. With a little patience (and maybe a dash of Impatiens) we can share these qualities and not feel so alone. We will never feel completely fulfilled and at peace on earth unless we do learn to share the life skills we have brought into the world.

Impatiens helps us accept that we all have an equal role in bringing the vision of a healed world into reality. It can foster our sense of belonging here, making earth feel like a place where we can relax and be truly at home.

POSSIBLE PHYSICAL IMBALANCES

Mental and physical tension can lead to many problems – indigestion through rushed eating, headaches and other body aches, insomnia and inability to relax. Constant activity makes us vulnerable to exhaustion and burn out. Vision problems and disorientative complaints may develop as a result of tension held in the head.

Some cases of infertility have responded well to Impatiens, where there was a need to slow down and become inwardly receptive to fertilisation. Don't forget that the father has equal responsibility here!

CLASSICAL USES

For a constant sense of urgency; for intolerance and impatience; for those for whom nothing happens fast enough; for the child who wants to be an adult now; for those who convert anger and frustration into busyness and hurry; for obsessively goal-oriented people; to help accept the natural pace of others; to help learn to enjoy the process and not just the result; to help develop trust in the world; to help find where you belong and just be there.

COMPLEMENTARY BACH FLOWERS

Elm — when commitments and deadlines become overwhelming.
Willow — when you become resentful of all the 'fools' (as you see it) you have to deal with to get the job done.
Cherry Plum — when things are right out of control and you don't know what will happen next.

SUPPORTIVE MEASURES

- Persevere with relaxation and meditation techniques, even though at first they may seem a totally unproductive and even painful waste of time. They could profoundly change your life.
- Investigate philosophies which will help you understand that the process is as important as the goal, and that everyone travels the path in their own way, but we are all travelling it together.
- Join a team!

Larch
(Larix decidua)

Positive state
tries for 'personal best'

Negative state
no attempt made, for fear of failure

If fear of failure is strong enough, failure usually occurs, or is avoided only because an attempt was never made. The negative Larch state can be a stagnant existence, in which one is repeatedly immobilised by fear. Creative capacities contract and depression develops. As Shakespeare said so long ago: 'Our doubts are traitors, and make us lose the good we oft might win, by fearing to attempt.'

What appears as downright stubbornness may in fact be a refusal rooted in fear of failure. Young children can illustrate this pattern well — refusing, for example, to read aloud in class for fear of failure and humiliation. Fear of this kind may also cause severe anticipatory anxiety before examinations or public speaking engagements, artistic or sporting performances, or before any situation which we feel will leave us exposed to the judgement of a group — even the family! We experience enormous self-doubt and lack of confidence about attempting anything new, such as taking on a new job or making a change of direction within an existing career. Any situation where we fear failure in attempting something important to us calls for Larch.

This remedy can help access our confidence in our own unique creative talents, giving us faith in our capacity to have an honest go. It can help us view setbacks and mistakes as valuable steps on the way to true mastery and direction in our lives. Larch helps move the emphasis away from the expectations and judgements of others, and towards the attempt to make a 'personal best' contribution to a better world.

POSSIBLE PHYSICAL IMBALANCES

Larch has a strong connection with the Throat Centre — the flower's position on the branch somewhat resembling the thyroid's attachment to the oesophagus. Thus we can expect that imbalances in this area – also manifesting as 'stifled' personal expression in life — will lead to anything from recurring sore throats and tonsillitis through to thyroid dysfunction and associated problems.

Larch also has an affinity for the Sacral Centre located in the pelvic basin — the source of our strongest creative energies. If an unbalanced Throat Centre has a restrictive influence on the natural upward flow of creative energy from the Sacral Centre, there may be congestive problems in the reproductive organs.

CLASSICAL USES

For fear of failure; for fear of public speaking, and for speech problems such as stuttering; for loss or lack of self-confidence; to encourage more creative self-expression; to encourage self-assertion; to encourage 'having a go'; to help achieve 'personal best' performances; to enhance self-appreciation of one's contribution to the world.

COMPLEMENTARY BACH FLOWERS

Elm — when fear of failure arises out of an overburden of responsibility.

Gentian — when fear and discouragement comes from repeated setbacks.

Willow — when unwillingness to have a go leads to resentment about the fact that things aren't proceeding the way you would like them to.

Walnut — when old attachments and influences (especially family ones) make self-assertion seem too risky and difficult.

SUPPORTIVE MEASURES

- Assertiveness and self-esteem courses will be invaluable, as will any that can help develop effective communication skills. Activities that free up your creative energies will be most valuable of all — psycho-drama, eurhythmics, singing, public speaking, dance and movement, or any other form of expression that interests you.

- Always choose a teacher or facilitator with whom you feel comfortable and secure. Spend as much time as you can in the company of those who will give you support and encouragement in ventures that develop confidence and creativity.

- Have a go! Nothing ventured, nothing gained!

Mimulus
(Mimulus guttatus)

Positive state
acceptance of life's inherent risks

Negative state
fearfulness and phobic states

Mimulus people in the negative state fear their own reactions to a particular situation or occurrence. They have a rational understanding of the external cause of their fear, but it does not help them to deal with its effect on them. This intense emotional reaction to certain possibilities, even well before the event, is frequently overpowering, and the response is to shy away from anxiety-producing areas. In this way, power is given away to the object of fear.

These fears are of known origin — of situations where we might be publicly humiliated, of poverty or failure in business, of sexual violation or physical violence, of plane or traffic accidents, of being exploited by those we trust. All these things are in fact possible, but when our fears severely restrict the whole of life, we should consider Mimulus.

This remedy helps restore personal freedom through an increased willingness to accept life's inherent risks and vulnerabilities, in this way giving us increased access to its abundant offerings also. The mimulus plant risks its future in the form of thousands of seeds to the water of a nearby stream. Some are washed away, it is true, but others lodge between the stones of the riverbank to begin new life. So it is that with the help of the remedy, we develop the inner security and strength that can allow us to risk experiencing life to the full, reaping its rewards in doing so.

POSSIBLE PHYSICAL IMBALANCES

Fear that is intense and held-in can eventually have a negative effect on the kidney/adrenals and bladder. Problems such as bed-wetting are also a possibility — a child may be inwardly fearful during the day, unconsciously 'holding on' until in sleep they let go with the inevitable result. Nervous tension and related problems are common, manifesting in conditions such as nervous stomach, dyspepsia and nervous bowel. Sinus problems may also occur – being overly effected by what or who's close.

CLASSICAL USES

For any fear of a known origin; for shyness, timidity and/or self-consciousness; for those who fear confrontation; for nervous dread of normal/everyday experiences; to improve self-confidence; for courage when facing everyday situations.

COMPLEMENTARY BACH FLOWERS

Cherry Plum — when intensity of emotion makes you fear you will do something drastic.

Rock Rose — when there is absolute terror!

Compare Mimulus with Aspen, which is for fears of unknown origin.

SUPPORTIVE MEASURES

- Mimulus people need to take refuge on a regular basis in their 'sanctuary' — it can be anything from a favourite cubbyhouse to a temple — if they are to safeguard their sensitive and delicate natures. This sense of sanctuary can also be created internally through meditation and relaxation techniques, or through creative visualisation.

- A balanced approach to diet and lifestyle is extremely important for the survival of those who are spiritually sensitive. Mimulus will help you tune in to the particular needs of mind and body in this regard.

Mustard
(Sinapis arvensis)

Positive state
understanding our 'dark' energies

Negative state
depression of unknown origin

In life's darkest moments, and in lives that are full of such moments, this flower essence can help. Mustard is useful in situations where, however frequently the darkness falls, we never have any conscious warning. It is a black hole that appears suddenly out of nowhere, and disappears just as fast. Women may experience it regularly during their monthly cycle without ever having a sense of being prepared, or it may come during certain seasons of the year. Because there is no feeling of impending gloom beforehand, it can make us feel like victims of a dark and unseen force from outside. Depression arrives suddenly, for a reason known only to our inner selves. Mustard can help put us in touch with this deeper self, its rhythms and energies. Knowing the darkness is temporary, we feel less trapped, and safer about facing this eruption of the Shadow side, even gaining some insight into its nature. These times do in fact provide great opportunities for soul-searching. As we acquire self-knowledge, mood changes become far less pronounced and more predictable. A more harmonious relationship between conscious and unconscious aspects of self is being established.

POSSIBLE PHYSICAL IMBALANCES

Think of Mustard for any illness that coincides with or directly follows the sudden onset of a depressed state. PMT could be included here.

CLASSICAL USES

For sudden depression and gloom for no apparent reason; for a history of sudden depressed states followed by equally sudden recoveries; to assist in developing a deeper understanding of self; to help us shine out in the world with the energy of our whole selves.

COMPLEMENTARY BACH FLOWERS

Cherry Plum — when life feels out of control.

Rock Rose — when the darkness is accompanied by terror.

Recue Remedy (which contains both Cherry Plum and Rock Rose) can be used as required in addition to Mustard.

Compare Mustard with Gorse and Gentian, which are for depressive states resulting from more obvious causes.

SUPPORTIVE MEASURES

- Therapies to develop self-awareness, such as dreamwork, psychotherapy, and meditation will be useful.

- Body-awareness is also helpful – yoga, tai chi, controlled breathing techniques etc.

- Study the Jungian concept of the Shadow, that largely unknown area of the psyche where much energy is stored.

- Take over and take the plunge inward, toward insight!

Oak
(Quercus robur)

Positive state
ability to take it easy sometimes

Negative state
life seen as intrinsically a struggle

'Life wasn't meant to be easy' is the motto by which the Oak person lives. Life is a constant struggle with no expectation that things could be easier, or that one deserves a better deal. There is no doubt that you can completely depend on Oak people to get a job done, but at what cost to them? Can they depend on themselves to extract any joy from life, or can they rely on their bodies to endure the impossible workload that has been taken on? There is a time when they come to realise that the answer is No!

The determination and optimism of Oak people in even the most hopeless situations is legendary, but eventually there is a price to pay. Lack of concern for personal well-being can mean that health is jeopardised to the point where they are unable to continue. But before this seemingly inevitable physical exhaustion and breakdown, Oak can help them direct their strength and determination towards their own healing. They may then acknowledge and act on the fact that they do need rest, that there is personal discomfort, or that there are some ordinary pleasures they have denied themselves for years. In the Oak person's new world order, complaints will be considered, and life will be allowed to become easy and enjoyable where possible. We all have a God-given right to take it easy when we need to, and Oak can help to reawaken this capacity.

POSSIBLE PHYSICAL IMBALANCES

Oak people often have strong constitutions, but over time they begin to develop signs of chronic structural fatigue such as rheumatic and arthritic pains and restrictions. Because they endure physical ailments silently, those around them are often unaware of their pain. It is usually only the cumulative effect of many ailments that forces them to seek help.

CLASSICAL USES

For the silent sufferer who plods on regardless; for the battler whose health finally falters after years of neglect; for those who never complain despite difficult circumstances; for the dependable 'draught-horse' type who is getting tired; to help feel more deserving of the good things life can offer; to help ask not what you can do for your country, but what your country can do for you!; to help enjoy life.

COMPLEMENTARY BACH FLOWERS

Elm — when there is an accompanying feeling of anxious overwhelm caused by the burdens of life.

Olive and/or Hornbeam — when there is exhaustion.

Rock Water — when there is extreme self-denial and self-martyrdom.

SUPPORTIVE MEASURES

- Try to ask for help, and learn to accept it.
- Put aside an hour or two of 'me' time every week, and spend it doing something you really want to do, for no other reason than your own enjoyment.
- Learn to ask yourself frequently, 'How do I feel?', so that you can tune in to your inner needs. Relaxation techniques and disciplines that encourage reflection will enhance this exploration.
- Take a break now!!

Olive

(Olea europaea)

Positive state
dynamic, energised

Negative state
energy reserves completely used up

Olive people in the negative state are exhausted on all levels – physically, emotionally, mentally and spiritually. Their complete lack of energy undermines any attempt to exert themselves in mind or body, and means in fact that their condition is actually made worse by thinking about it. Any exercise of the will is short-lived, and they are slow to recover.

Think of Olive for exhaustion resulting from prolonged periods of stress on both mental and physical levels, such as that experienced by a mother with her first baby (or her eighth!), or during and immediately after examinations or intense work periods. Use it as support during intensive training for any event requiring endurance and quick recovery, and for all situations that place an excessive demand on mental and physical resources.

Olive helps restore vitality at the very deep level at which energy and inspiration has its source. When energy is dissipated or lost over a period of time for whatever reason, Olive can help strengthen and reintegrate the subtle energetic bodies, restoring to us our dynamic presence in the world.

POSSIBLE PHYSICAL IMBALANCES

Physical fatigue is always present in the negative Olive state. Natural immunity is prone to breakdown, leaving us susceptible to infection, and proper recovery from illness is hampered by being severely run down in the first place. Think of Olive for assisting all rehabilitation processes, and for recovery from strenuous activity, physical trauma or prolonged stress.

CLASSICAL USES

For convalescents; for rehabilitation after an incapacitating accident; for physical and mental exhaustion; for insomnia from overtiredness; as a support during times when endurance is tested; to help increase resilience.

COMPLEMENTARY BACH FLOWERS

Hornbeam — when there is extreme mental fatigue, to enhance and support the action of Olive.

Wild Rose — when there is apathy and a tendency to become withdrawn.

Impatiens — when there is impatience with the recovery process.

SUPPORTIVE MEASURES

- Rest at every opportunity – sleep if possible. Learn to integrate more relaxation and play into your life.
- Engage in energising but not exhausting activities — gentle aerobics, walking etc. Meditation and relaxation techniques which strengthen both body and soul will be very useful.
- Maintain a healthy and nutritious diet.

Pine
(Pinus sylvestris)

Positive state
self-forgiveness

Negative state
stuck in regret about past failure
guilt/self-reproach

Pine people in the negative state regret the past, and so continue to hold onto it in the hope that it may change. However, all that can be changed about the past is our attitude towards it, and if this does not happen, we condemn ourselves to a life of guilt and self-reproach. How can we succeed in the present if we are constantly reliving past failures?

In the hope of undoing past imperfections, we may adopt a perfectionist approach now, setting ourselves unrealistically high standards and goals. The consequence of aiming so high is to fall short, reinforcing feelings of failure and guilt over letting ourselves and others down.

Pine helps develop a positive view of the past, enabling us to see so-called mistakes and indiscretions as simply points on a learning curve. An 'imperfect score' can be a wonderful opportunity to refine skills and abilities, in a life-long process that has endless possibilities. Pine helps reawaken the sense of inner perfection so often lost during life's trials.

POSSIBLE PHYSICAL IMBALANCES

As pine self-reproach 'eats away' at the mind, the body often follows in sympathy. Chronic inflammatory conditions, sometimes of an auto-immune nature, can easily develop as rheumatic complaints or digestive tract complaints especially of the bowel — an area which can symbolise the ability to let go of the past.

CLASSICAL USES

For the over-dutiful person who feels guilt-ridden over some failure of obligation; for those who easily take responsibility for the failings of others; for the self-reproachful perfectionist; for strong feelings of guilt; to help let yourself off the hook.

COMPLEMENTARY BACH FLOWERS

Willow — when there is also a feeling of resentment towards the object of guilt. (Guilt is often regarded as resentment turned inward.)

Larch — when fear of future failure arises from dwelling on past failures.

Walnut and/or Honeysuckle — When there is strong emotional attachment to past beliefs and relationships.

SUPPORTIVE MEASURES

- Practise forgiveness of self and others – through counselling, meditative disciplines or any other means available to you. This will enable you to view your life with more balance and optimism.
- Work to construct an environment — family, friends, occupation — that will give appreciation, respect and reinforcement to your talents and abilities.
- Serve yourself as you would serve others.

Red Chestnut

(Aesculus carnea)

Positive state
objective about welfare of loved ones

Negative state
over-fearful for others

Red Chestnut people in the negative state, with their overactive and outwardly-directed Heart Centre energies, become too concerned and fearful for the welfare of others. There is a need to develop a healthier balance between self-concern and concern for others, so that the heart's focus is not all outside the self.

An example of this state can be seen in excessively anxious parents who feel continual fear for their children's safety when they are not close by. Thoughts are constantly focused on the worst that may happen to friends and loved ones. Anticipatory anxiety may become a self-fulfilling prophecy as they wait for the worst, and in their minds inevitable, outcome. When the child returns home from school safely, the husband or wife returns from work without being involved in a car accident, or when a close friend makes contact after an absence from the social scene, Red Chestnut people feel great relief.

This remedy helps heal the heart and soothe excessive anxiety. It allows us to step back far enough from mental and emotional participation in others' real or potential troubles to be of objective help. Then we can be free to empathise with those close to us without losing our sense of proportion and personal power.

POSSIBLE PHYSICAL IMBALANCES

With all that heart energy being directed outwards, the immunity of Red Chestnut people to surrounding stressful influences can easily become depleted. Burn out, both physical and emotional, and increased susceptibility to illness are common occurrences. Red Chestnut helps to develop a protective auric seal around the self.

CLASSICAL USES

For projection of fear onto others; for the anxious, over-protective parent or friend; for the co-dependent health practitioner, social worker etc., overly concerned about clients' welfare; for the over-sympathetic person who finds another's slightest distress gut-wrenching; to transform with empathy rather than stagnate with sympathy.

COMPLEMENTARY BACH FLOWERS

Walnut — when extreme emotional attachment clouds one's better judgement and objectivity in relationships.

Cherry Plum — when you fear that the situation will be out of your control.

Aspen — when there is a fear of the unknown.

Mimulus — when the fear for another is about something specific.

SUPPORTIVE MEASURES

- Meditation, creative visualisation, yoga and tai chi will help centre and direct your energies, developing true spiritual Self-consciousness.

- Learn to enjoy spending some time alone, and create more personal space for yourself in the home, at work etc.

- Get to know yourself and your own special needs.

Rock Rose

(Helianthemum nummularium)

Positive state
confident calm

Negative state
panic and terror

The key element of the negative Rock Rose state is terror that consumes the mind, sending it into panic and chaos. Feelings of terror may be tucked away in the unconscious, to be released when the conditions are right, and then a child or adult wakes from a horrible nightmare frozen with fear, or an expectant first-time mother suddenly feels terror when she contemplates labour and early motherhood. A war veteran may relive combat and the absolute terror that was not fully experienced at the time. Rock Rose can help alleviate terror in anticipation of future events too – examinations, public performances, losing a job, having your worst nightmare come true in some way.

The plant's bright yellow flowers, radiating gold from the centre, reflect its role in bringing mental clarity and a peaceful heart. It helps us transcend terror and shine through during life's frightening initiations. Without the inhibiting effects of fear, full potential can be lived, and our true colours can shine through, leaving us at peace with ourselves and the world.

POSSIBLE PHYSICAL IMBALANCES

Rock Rose people in the negative state may be prone to nervous digestive disorders – the stomach is the area that reflects how we 'greet' the next moment in time. The remedy can be a useful supportive measure during the treatment of acute physical problems such as asthma attacks when anxiety is pronounced. Adrenal fatigue may develop because of this area's role in the body's fear-response.

CLASSICAL USES

For terror attacks and nightmares; for adrenal fatigue in the thrill-seeker or continuous big event performer; for extreme anticipatory anxiety; to help develop the courage to shine through life's challenges.

COMPLEMENTARY BACH FLOWERS

Rock Rose is an important ingredient in Rescue Remedy, whose profound and multi-purpose usefulness results from individual and synergistic effects of the remedies it contains. Think of Rescue Remedy in all emergency situations.

SUPPORTIVE MEASURES

- Learn techniques that will help bring mental calm and control, such as controlled breathing, relaxation and meditation, yoga and tai chi. Martial arts may, in addition, increase self-confidence for those who feel very vulnerable in the world.
- Consider receiving some professional counselling.
- Try grounding yourself through exercise, gardening etc.
- Creative visualisation should be considered as one of a range of techniques used to protect the Solar Plexus – the centre where the experience of terror is focused.

Rock Water

(Spring or well water known for its healing qualities)

Positive state
flexibility, adaptability

Negative state
rigid obsession with ideals

Rock Water people in the negative state place a rigid external ideal or set of beliefs before their own internal needs. For the sake of a way of living that has idealistic appeal they will sacrifice and deny desires and feelings. Unfortunately this behaviour is often viewed by others as self-righteous martyrdom, serving only to alienate them and their cause from family, friends and associates.

A classic Rock Water case history can look like this. A client comes with major concerns about his general health. He describes to me his daily routine – up at exactly 6.02 a.m., beginning the day with 20 minutes' meditation; at 6.22 a.m. a 15-minute brisk walk; at 6.37 a.m. a bowel movement until complete evacuation takes place (the quality of the whole day being dependent on this process); breakfast is a large bowl of muesli made from exactly weighed amounts of raw ingredients — the recipe coming from the book that also outlines the rest of his regime — and so on, until bedtime at precisely 10.02 p.m. Needless to say this textbook lifestyle takes more out of him than it puts back. He, and to a lesser extent everyone around him, has become a victim of his own rigid regimentation. He has given up all his freedoms in pursuit of a way of life that has worked beautifully for someone else.

Rock Water can help this person let go of much of his obsessive behaviour, developing a more flexible approach that can accommodate spontaneous needs and desires, in this way making a place for enjoyment and pleasure.

POSSIBLE PHYSICAL IMBALANCES

The rigid mental make-up of the negative Rock Water state will eventually manifest structurally in the body. A range of complaints from muscular tension and stiffness through to arthritic conditions commonly develop. Headaches — the head aching to follow the heart — are also common. Behaviours involving loss of control after over-control in the negative state, such as binge-eating after long periods of dieting, may be a pattern.

CLASSICAL USES

For the perfectionist; for the martyr who sacrifices self as an example to all; for the fanatical idealist; for the workaholic; for the creature of habit; to enhance flexibility and adaptability; to help us to start enjoying life.

COMPLEMENTARY BACH FLOWERS

Vervain — when there is a desire to change others to our way of thinking.

Beech — when there is intolerance of others who think differently.

SUPPORTIVE MEASURES

- Take a holiday!

- Engage in physical exercise that improves suppleness, such as flexing and stretching exercises, yoga, tai chi, and other disciplines that increase body-awareness.

- During the day, ask yourself regularly, 'How do I feel about this?' and try to follow your instinct whenever possible.

Scleranthus
(Scleranthus annus)

Positive state
clear feeling for the 'right' decision

Negative state
Torn between two opposites
Everyday Indecision

Scleranthus people in the negative state have great difficulty deciding between what seem like two opposing options. This lack of confidence in their own judgement may make them so hesitant that the opportunity for decision completely passes them by. Even worse, someone else may feel obliged to make the decision for them. Either way they are left feeling powerless to influence life-direction and quality. Sometimes no decision is required at a given moment, but still we agonise, creating confusion and imbalance, within and without.

This kind of wavering can result from tension between an adaptive, feeling-based way of being, and one that places emphasis on controlled, mental decision-making. Do we choose clothes the night before we need to wear them, and worry that the weather may not suit, or do we leave the decision till morning and see what the day is like? At home or at work, do we make a monumental issue out of choosing between two jobs, both of which are urgent, or do we do the one we actually feel like doing, completing it quickly and with little effort?

Scleranthus can help us differentiate between those situations in which we need to make it happen, and those in which we can just let it happen. By raising our awareness of what feels appropriate, we begin to know instinctively which option has right of way. Scleranthus helps create a healthy equilibrium between inner feeling and outer action, in this way bringing balance to our lives.

POSSIBLE PHYSICAL IMBALANCES

Imbalance and vacillation can easily manifest at the physical level as hormone imbalance, particularly as a result of thyroid dysfunction. The thyroid is conditioned by the Throat Centre, which relates to qualities of self-assertion and outward responsiveness to life. Consider Scleranthus for any condition that includes cyclical or changeable physical symptoms.

CLASSICAL USES

For dramatic mood-swings; for constant hesitancy and indecisiveness; for persistent states of mental confusion; for extreme dependency on others for decision-making; for co-dependent relationships in which one partner is always the one rescued from the consequences of his or her mistakes: to help calmly know when to retreat or when to advance.

COMPLEMENTARY BACH FLOWERS

Walnut — when emotional attachment clouds the ability to make a decision.

Larch — when fear of failure causes hesitancy in decision-making.
Mimulus — when there is fear of the consequences of a decision.

SUPPORTIVE MEASURES

- Try to be more aware of which opposing extremes are creating tension and imbalance in your life. Start a diary that will help you gain an overview of the day's ups and downs. Become more aware of cyclic patterns — physical, mental and emotional — so that instead of being their victim you can use them in practical and productive ways. When you are on a physical high, make the most of it. When emotional energy is low, choose activities that will help ground and centre you.

- Remember, if you cannot make up your mind, see what your heart says!

Star of Bethlehem

(Ornithogalum umbellatum)

Positive state
body and soul work together for healing

Negative state
after-effects of shock/trauma

When we are thrown into disarray by some shock — after bad news or an accident, after a general anaesthetic, after falling victim to physical or emotional violence, after childbirth or other prolonged stress, even where these things occurred many years ago, think of Star of Bethlehem. After such experiences, the 'subtle' bodies – the level at which our thoughts and emotions exist — are seriously disturbed and shaken out of harmony. This remedy can help guide the body-mind back into alignment after trauma so that healing takes place in a smoother and more profound way, at the level of the subtle anatomy.

The whiteness of Star of Bethlehem signifies its role in helping to amplify the protective white light of the universe in us, while the configuration of the flower – a star made of two triangles, one pointing up and the other down – symbolises the balanced merging of heaven and earth, and in this case the merging of body and soul. Under the soul's reconnecting influence the body truly becomes a temple of the spirit.

POSSIBLE PHYSICAL IMBALANCES

The stomach often bears the brunt of shock both during and after trauma. Its condition reflects how we take in experience. If there is unresolved shock in the system, we may live in conscious or unconscious anticipation of re-experiencing the original trauma — we are eaten up with worry about how to control the future, and become vulnerable to stomach ulceration, internal spasm or guarding etc.

CLASSICAL USES

For past or recent shock and trauma; for the after-effects of surgery and anaesthetics; for the effects of physical or emotional violation; for the effects of prolonged stress; to support psychotherapy and regression therapies which involve re-experience of past trauma.

COMPLEMENTARY BACH FLOWERS

Rock Rose — when there is panic and terror. Rock Rose and Star of Bethlehem are both ingredients of Rescue Remedy.

Mimulus — when strong fears develop related to traumatic experience.

Walnut — when extreme sensitivity makes us more vulnerable to shock and trauma.

SUPPORTIVE MEASURES

- Professional guidance is often appropriate in situations calling for the use of Star of Bethlehem.
- Learn methods of self-protection, for example visualising protective white light, especially in the Solar Plexus area.
- Learn to sense and recognise places and circumstances where you don't feel safe, and either avoid them or take protective precautions.
- Give yourself adequate nurturing and recovery time after experiencing shock of any kind.

Sweet Chestnut

(Castanea sativa)

Positive state
irrepressible resilience

Negative state
end of endurance – the 'last straw'

When life has taken us to the limits of our endurance and we simply cannot and will not take any more, Sweet Chestnut can help us climb out of the depths of despair into a new and easier era. It can act as a catalyst in making the transition from the Piscean consciousness of 'dying in order to live', to the Aquarian consciousness of growth that unfolds more easily and with less pain. Sweet Chestnut may help bring about the demise of the 'no pain, no gain' philosophy!

This remedy can be helpful at times like mid-life, menopause, or the end of a long, arduous and demanding course of study, when long-term stress reaches crisis point. It can be for those desperate but enlightening moments of utter despair when you vow you will never, never do something this way again — the only way out of here is up!

Sweet Chestnut helps restore dignity, strength and self-assurance — qualities abundantly displayed in the powerful presence of a tree that can live a thousand years. Even the deeply furrowed bark reminds us of the skin of an old and wise person who has been through it all and still stands strong and vital. When the flowers light up the tree we are reminded of our irrepressible resilience.

POSSIBLE PHYSICAL IMBALANCES

Sweet Chestnut can help at those crisis points when we have carried an illness for a long time, but can do so no longer without special support and attention. It can be used in terminal illness or for those on the threshold of death, to help achieve a more peaceful and serene disposition. The deep despair associated with the physically incapacitating aftermath of trauma such as spinal injuries and strokes may also call for Sweet Chestnut.

CLASSICAL USES

For 'the straw that breaks the camel's back'; for deep despair; for the symbolic deaths in our lives — and the rebirths; to give a chance for peace of mind.

COMPLEMENTARY BACH FLOWERS

Olive — when there is complete mental and physical exhaustion. (Compare Hornbeam, where fatigue is more mental.)

Elm — when we are completely overwhelmed by responsibility.

Rescue Remedy — should be considered as well as, or instead of, Sweet Chestnut.

SUPPORTIVE MEASURES

- Seek professional guidance and support.
- When things reach such a low ebb, a complete re-evaluation and re-assessment of your life is valuable. Vocational guidance will be useful.
- A healthy diet and lifestyle is especially important at this time.

Vervain
(Verbena officinalis)

Positive state
accepts validity of other spiritual paths

Negative state
desire to convert others

Vervain helps moderate that part of us that desperately wants to convert everybody else to our way of thinking. This is a frightening energy in the unbalanced Vervain person – most of the atrocities that have occurred 'in the name of God' are the result of an extreme Vervain state. The process goes something like this – we pluck a beautiful and profound piece of spiritual insight from the collective consciousness, then in order to communicate it to others, we adapt it to fit the confines of our culture and limited intelligence. We then try to force this very contrived artefact on everyone we meet, because we want so badly to pass on the flash we have received. But whether others accept our message or not, there is a loss. Even those who are all too ready to believe are not given the experience, but only our distorted retelling of it, and those who don't react with enthusiasm are subject to our rage at their denial of the 'Truth'.

Vervain helps us realise it is possible to actively inspire and passively provide space for others to reach actualisation on their own unique life-paths, without invading them. In the quest to awaken and spiritually unite with the divine Beloved in another or others, we often succeed only in invasion of this kind, not having completed the necessary earthly groundwork. The vervain plant has a tough and erect branching habit, spear-like in its aspiration for greater height and spiritual penetration, but each branch, while remaining joined at the root, grows individually towards the heavens.

By helping us become more secure in our own beliefs and their basis in inner experience, we become able to see the possibility of truths in other ideologies. Vervain people in the positive state do not lose their enthusiasm and perseverance — they will die for their cause if need be — but that cause is no longer narrow and insular, and does not claim to have all the answers.

POSSIBLE PHYSICAL IMBALANCES

Nervous and muscular tension is an almost standard result of an overzealous approach to life. Inability to relax — the cause will not allow it — can mean a predisposition to heart problems. Ungrounded idealism can lead to a loss of connection with the body and its needs. Digestive complaints are common.

CLASSICAL USES

For the over-enthusiastic healer; for the bible-basher; for blind faith fanatics; for the martyr for a cause; for those who invade the personal space of others; for discarnate, ungrounded states; to help learn to ride with rather than override others; to remind us that we teach best what we need to learn ourselves.

COMPLEMENTARY BACH FLOWERS

Beech — when there is intolerance of the views of others.
Rock Water — when there is a strong impulse towards self-denial.
Walnut — when belief-systems are received and controlled from outside.

SUPPORTIVE MEASURES

- Relax and take a holiday from the cause.
- Try to incorporate passive and introverted activities such as relaxation techniques, meditation, or just quality time on your own doing things you enjoy – reading, going to the movies or taking a stroll in the park. This may help restore balance to an exclusively extroverted life.

Vine

(Vitis vinifera)

Positive state
will to dominate becomes will to co-operate

Negative state
might is right — will to dominate

Vine people in the negative state only know one way — their way! — and they nearly always have the strength of will to get it — unless they meet another Vine person! These people are strong, assertive, decisive and self-sufficient, and because their way has been so successful, they believe they can impose it on everyone else. Their will to power can mean that they use others as stepping stones to increase their own stature, just as the vine uses the branches of a host plant to pull itself up.

In order to reach wholeness and balance, Vine people need to recognise their genuine need of others, not just as a means to an end. Eventually we cannot draw those we care about to us by will alone, nor does it bring us an easy conscience or peace of mind to do so. It is time to allow the heart's softening, springtime energy to flower, and the plant's green blossoms symbolise this occurrence.

In the positive state, Vine people are capable of heart-felt compassion, and combined with their strong will and commitment, this makes them formidable exponents of good in the world. They are natural leaders, and when the heart's influence transforms the desire to dominate into a desire to co-operate, they become inspirational, supportive, dependable, and flexible enough to respond to the needs of others as well as their own.

POSSIBLE PHYSICAL IMBALANCES

Flexibility is a key issue for Vine people. On a physical level, their bodies tend to display it less as they get older. They may experience anything from simple tension to 'frozen' structural forms of arthritis. Hardening of the circulatory vessels can occur, leading to heart problems and other complaints of the circulatory system.

CLASSICAL USES

For people who use expressions like 'I'm the boss!' 'Do it because I say so!' 'Let me steer!' 'It's my way or the highway!'; for those who are stuck in their own ways; to help loosen up and let life happen.

COMPLEMENTARY BACH FLOWERS

Beech — when there is intolerance of the views of others.
Chicory — wants to own the rights to you.
Rock Water — when there is a strong impulse towards self-denial.
Vervain — wants to convert everybody to their way of thinking.
Vine — wants dominance.

SUPPORTIVE MEASURES

- Becoming involved in voluntary community work may be rewarding:
  a) because you are accepting rather than making demands.
  b) because it is work that involves the heart.

- Any activity that increases physical suppleness is beneficial to well-being on all levels.

- Even if you think you are an old dog, try to learn new tricks!

Walnut
(Juglans regia)

Positive state
inner knowledge of next step in life-path

Negative state
deflected from path by influence of others

When we are too easily influenced by others to be able to determine our own true destinies, Walnut is the Bach Flower to consider. There are times of major transition in all our lives — teething, first separation from parents, puberty, loss of loved ones, mid-life, menopause etc., when we are very vulnerable to outside influences. These may be those of individuals or groups wanting to 'convert' us, or the call of safe, familiar patterns. In either case, part of us longs to follow them with all our heart, while another part knows this is wrong for us or a backward step. Dr Bach called this remedy the link-breaker, because of its role in breaking emotional ties and habits that do not serve the whole self.

When opened, the walnut resembles a brain — the centre which allows us to make head-based rather than heart-based decisions when necessary. The tree gives off chemical signals to other plants and animals, deterring them from coming too close. This symbolises the way Walnut can help create enough protected space for us to negotiate the internal changes necessary for the next stage of growth without being unduly influenced by those around us.

POSSIBLE PHYSICAL IMBALANCES

Over-sensitivity to outside influences applies to the physical environment also. Sensitivities to pollen and air-borne pollutants, and multiple food sensitivities are common. In its capacity as protector of the Heart Centre, Walnut helps improve natural immunity, especially against recurring infection, due to its influence on the thymus gland, which is associated with the Heart Centre. Walnut's role in the treatment of auto-immune disease will become more evident as time goes on.

CLASSICAL USES

The 'link-breaker'; for fear of separation; for loss of a loved one; for over-attachment to family, friends, peer group etc.; for over-sensitivity to the environment — physical, mental or emotional; to help improve general immunity; to help let go — loved ones, clients, old habits.

COMPLEMENTARY BACH FLOWERS

Walnut complements and enhances the action of all the other Bach Flowers.

SUPPORTIVE MEASURES

- Calling in a third emotionally objective party is often very useful in conflicts and problems arising out of 'Walnut' situations.
- Use creative visualisation to protect the Heart Centre and Solar Plexus.
- Write down the pros and cons of the situation you find yourself in. This will allow you to make a more objective appraisal of the direction you need to take.
- Create your own safe place of retreat and go there in body or in spirit when you need to.

Water Violet

(Hottonia palustris)

Positive state
comfortable connection with others

Negative state
aloof and cut off from others

Just as the plant is unapproachable in its watery habitat, so Water Violet people in the negative state are unapproachable and aloof. All of us are drawn to seclusion and privacy to some extent — after all, one of the reasons we are here is to experience our spirits as separate entities in physical bodies. Most of the time, however, we seek balance between involvement and non-involvement, between association and dissociation, between committed and uncommitted relationship. It is when our lives have become biased towards insularity and detachment and we begin to feel a lack in our hearts that Water Violet can ameliorate.

Water Violet people have a highly spiritual and delicate nature of which they are as proud as they are protective. Their artistic talents often bring them the material rewards that will assure their independence, so that the desire to be alone is easily satisfied. But it can be cold comfort to the heart, which longs to merge with others, recognising that at a feeling level, their needs and concerns are ours also. Water Violet can help soften the impact of personal exchange on the heart, much as water acts as a buffer between the plant and its earth connection, leaving the delicate spirit intact and pure.

POSSIBLE PHYSICAL IMBALANCES

Water Violet people like to keep everything, including illness, 'close to the chest'. Asking for help is not their style – working it out internally is. When Heart Centre energies have to battle for full expression in this way, heart problems on a physical level can eventually develop.

CLASSICAL USES

For the aloof loner; for those too proud to ask for help; for those with a 'stiff upper lip'; for the arrogant, self-exiled outsider; to help become involved and feel part of it all; to help find it easier to join in.

COMPLEMENTARY BACH FLOWERS

Impatiens— when there is impatience with those wishing to come close.

SUPPORTIVE MEASURES

- Take a few risks with your independence — join a group, team or association that you know treats its members with respect. You may enjoy the interaction.
- Try socialising a bit more.
- Discover what it is that awakens your passion for life.
- Fall in love!

White Chestnut

(Aesculus hippocastanum)

Positive state
dynamic stillness of the mind

Negative state
unwanted thoughts

White Chestnut helps ease the mind away from its relentless search for thoughts that will resolve themselves into peace and satisfaction. Such a resolution cannot occur, as it could only take the form of no-thought, and so the mind goes into a spiral, chasing its own tail. Unwanted thoughts harass, torment and eventually exhaust the thinker, who feels like their victim.

Our minds, when they are so cluttered with thought that we are unable to concentrate, leave us easily distracted and prone to going off at a tangent. We may become obsessively worried about the past, or about tomorrow's important meeting. Mental arguments with people we haven't even met may run out of control. We are preoccupied by recurring thoughts that allow neither sleep nor effective concentration, persisting to the point where the head hurts. We crave a moment of mental calm.

Too much work, or simply becoming disconnected from the feeling-nature may propel us into the negative White Chestnut state. We should consider its use if we want relief from the pain and strain of thought congestion. This remedy can help release the mind from its addiction to constant thought, bringing new calm and clarity. We become more able to respond to feelings in a spontaneous yet poised manner, achieving an open and dynamic stillness of the mind.

POSSIBLE PHYSICAL IMBALANCES

Ailments from a congested head area are common — headache, migraine, sinus problems, recurring head colds, and even skin complaints on the head. Vision problems may also develop, and there is often tension in the head, neck and shoulder area. Spleen (which often needs to be vented) and stomach problems are not uncommon.

CLASSICAL USES

For insomnia due to an active mind; for constant worry; for persistent unwanted thoughts; for those who are overly analytical and unduly mentally oriented; for inability to concentrate; for exhaustion from an overactive mind; to help unwind and switch off mentally; to help one feel and not just think.

COMPLEMENTARY BACH FLOWERS

Olive — when there is mental and physical exhaustion.

Walnut — when recurring thoughts relate to a strong emotional attachment.

Mimulus — when there is fear associated with persistent thoughts.

Pine — when there is guilt associated with persistent thoughts.

SUPPORTIVE MEASURES

- Learn meditation and relaxation techniques.
- Regular physical activity will help swing the balance away from overemphasis on the mental sphere. Gardening and other manual work can have the same effect.
- Yoga, tai chi and other physical disciplines are also relaxing and mentally calming. Try walking!

Wild Oat

(Bromus ramosus)

Positive state
knowledge of true vocation

Negative state
unable to choose one of many paths

Wild Oat is the vocational guide for the soul. When we are unsure which of many directions to take as our true path in life, we should think of this remedy. Wild Oat people in the negative state are always searching for the job or way of life that feels the most authentic and valuable. They change careers, lifestyles, departments, but never feel they have found their niche or that they really belong.

The sense of belonging has to be found first of all within us if it is to be real and lasting. Wild Oat can help us make the committed connection to the world that is a prerequisite to clarity about direction. We must become truly involved in the game of life if we are to see what position we can best play, and in this way share the prize of achieving a common purpose.

When we lose our bearings, Wild Oat can help put us back on track towards self-realisation and fulfilment.

POSSIBLE PHYSICAL IMBALANCES

Job dissatisfaction often has associated specific or non-specific illness. Physical symptoms may also result from periods of depression. The immune system may be depressed.

CLASSICAL USES

For the 'Jack of all trades and master of none'; for the drifter; for those desiring a change of direction; for mid-life crisis; for vocational crisis; for adolescent apathy; to help prioritise and redefine future directions; to help steer us through life's bum steers; to help us hear our calling.

COMPLEMENTARY BACH FLOWERS

Compare Wild Oat with Scleranthus, which has difficulty in choosing between two possibilities.
Walnut — when emotional attachment clouds our vision of new directions.
Other remedies will naturally follow on from Wild Oat after some focus is achieved.

SUPPORTIVE MEASURES

- Vocational counselling and any other measures that enhance self-knowledge will be useful.

- Join in team or group activities that involve working towards a common goal.

- Remember you must lose sight of the shore before you can see new horizons.

Wild Rose

(Rosa canina)

Positive state

passion for life
involved

Negative state

withdrawn resignation

In the negative state, Wild Rose people withdraw from full participation in life. They are resigned to being an effect rather than a cause, and so they often find themselves stuck in a way of life that was designed around someone else's needs. Apathetic detachment is the only response they know how to make to this situation.

When we are lacking in motivation, and find ourselves saying things like, 'What's the use? There's no future for me, or no point in trying for one anyway', it is time to consider Wild Rose. We may have encountered a few setbacks, or experienced an illness that lasted longer than expected. As a result we have become dispirited, resigned to the notion that things will never get better.

When we have become ungrounded and discarnate in this way, Wild Rose can bring back our passionate involvement with life. Like other members of the rose family, these plants have a very strong and hardy root system that is grounded deeply, and securely attached to the earth. This remedy can be our teacher, helping us put our hearts back into living, and so restoring inner joy, vitality and enthusiasm.

POSSIBLE PHYSICAL IMBALANCES

Wild Rose is often useful in the treatment of long term or chronic illness. In the negative state, the 'disconnection' that occurs in the Heart Centre means that circulatory problems can arise. Coldness of extremities, decreased cerebral blood-flow leading to brain fag and vagueness, and low blood pressure are common. Fatigue and psychosomatic illness can also occur. Anecdotal evidence suggests that it may be useful in some cases of infertility, especially where a woman has 'lost faith' after trying to conceive for some time.

CLASSICAL USES

For pathological apathy; for withdrawal from life; for complete lack of interest in one's surroundings; for lack of perseverance through loss of motivation; to restore enthusiasm and passion for life; to help those who are 'not really here' become grounded in the present.

COMPLEMENTARY BACH FLOWERS

There are many Bach Flowers that will follow well the energising effect of Wild Rose. This remedy can be a catalyst for profound change.

SUPPORTIVE MEASURES

- Develop a daily routine and avoid oversleeping. Also, avoid prolonged meditation — a good balance of vigorous physical exercise is needed.
- Body-work and other somatic therapies will be very useful.
- Find out what it is that excites your passion and lust for life!

Willow
(Salix vitellina)

Positive state
responsible for own reality
emotional resilience

Negative state
blames the universe

'Why does this always happen to me? How come I always get a raw deal? I do the right thing, and look what happens — I miss out again!' 'It's no wonder I've got an attitude problem when life treats me like dirt. I never asked to be born anyway!' ... 'I know I could turn these feelings around by taking Bach Flowers, but I'd just like to wallow in my negative Willow state a bit longer!'

We all go through times when we feel like this — some of us (including yours truly) more than others. Society is full of the victim mentality, and as individuals we deal with it in ourselves and others every day. But we have to face the fact that a negative attitude can easily create a negative reality. On the days when we wake up in a bad mood, we are more likely to stub a toe getting out of bed. If we go to work in a foul temper, we are more likely to encounter hostility from colleagues. If we don't want to be wherever we are, we limit our possibilities of enjoyment. If, on the other hand, we have a positive outlook, we will naturally see and experience more of life's positive aspects.

Creating a positive outlook, though, is easier said than done. The tree's highly flexible branches symbolise the help this remedy can give us. It helps develop the potential we all have to be flexible and resilient enough to turn a negative attitude into a positive one. The bright yellow of its bare stems in the winter landscape symbolise the way our minds can be uplifted by the creative power of thought. Willow helps us to define and choose a more positive reality, in a powerful affirmation of life.

POSSIBLE PHYSICAL IMBALANCES

Conditions affecting the body's flexibility may develop — chronic tension, lack of suppleness, and arthritis. Headaches, especially migraine, often form part of the negative Willow picture. Fluid retention and bowel problems may reflect difficulty in letting go of negativity. For the most part, society supports the notion that we are victims of illness. Willow is therefore an important remedy for these times.

CLASSICAL USES

For feelings of bitterness and resentment; for 'attitude' problems; for those who blame others; for those who have difficulty taking responsibility for their lives; to help release pain, hurt and sadness; to improve mental flexibility and resilience, and therefore adaptability; to help uplift the mind.

COMPLEMENTARY BACH FLOWERS

Holly — when there are feelings of vengefulness towards those you feel have injured you.

Hornbeam — when you are weary and weighed down by the weight of your wet blanket.

SUPPORTIVE MEASURES

- Think about the idea that we create our own reality by our thoughts, beliefs and attitudes. Learn about the concept of karma.
- Make sure you give plenty of time and space to those aspects of your life where you do find enjoyment.
- Keep your body as supple as possible — some of the effects will spill over to the mind.
- Learn to take responsibility for what happens in your life. Even if you begin by doing it after the event, you will be learning how to react before the event, and so be in a better position to make changes.

RESCUE REMEDY

(Star of Bethlehem, Rock Rose, Impatiens, Clematis and Cherry Plum in combination.)

'When all else fails, or nothing else prevails.'

This jewel of Bach Flower combinations was the product of Dr Bach's intuitive genius. A perfect blend of qualities makes it the most potent and yet most gentle of all remedy combinations. Its multi-faceted nature makes it accessible to the Selective Sensitivity of all humanity. Rescue Remedy will help in all emergencies. It will give support in accident and trauma, and will help bring calm when there is fear and panic. It will help soothe the shell-shocked, settle the hysterical, consolidate the shattered, centre the disorientated. Rescue Remedy has a place in all homes.

OTHER COMBINED REMEDIES:

Combining more than four Bach Flowers is sometimes appropriate when prescribing for very general emotional or mental states. It is unlikely that all remedies in combinations such as this will elicit equally selectively sensitive responses, but they will have an overall effect. To use Rescue Remedy as an example, we might use it to help regain calm in a situation of panic, but would later choose a specific remedy based on personality type to stop a recurrence of the fear.

For further information on courses (including by correspondence), seminars, workshops and private consultations, contact:

Mark Wells

c/o Wells Naturopathic Centre

P.O. Box 79
Kew East VIC 3102
Australia

Mobile: 0409 985 970

www.wellsnaturopathy.com.au

Index

acne 12, 29
addictions 12, 23
adolescent apathy 88
adrenal complaints 14, 67, 68
advice-seeker 20
aloof and cut off from others 83
anaesthetics, effects of 28, 74
anxiety 32, 51, 55, 65, 67, 68
apathy 62, 88, 90
approval-seeker 32
arthritis 59, 70, 80, 92
asthma, support for treatment of 67
attention-seeking 26, 39
bed-wetting 56
binge-eating 70
bitterness and blaming 26, 92
body odour 29
bowel problems 56, 63, 92
brain fag 89
burn out 16, 45, 48, 66
cataract 37
circulatory problems 14, 80, 89
clinginess 25
co-dependent relationships 66, 72
combined remedies 7, 9, 93
concentration span, short 23, 24, 28
concussion 28
confidence, lack of 20, 51, 68, 71
confusion 71, 72
convalescents 62
convert others, desire to 77
crisis point 31, 75, 76, 88

cyclical or changeable symptoms 72
daydreamers 28
denies needs, desires and feelings
 32, 69, 77
dependent on others 18, 27, 28, 72
depression 36, 38, 58
despair 37, 75, 76
details, obsessed by 29, 30, 39
digestive complaints 12, 18, 22, 48,
 56, 63, 67, 73, 78
direction, unsure of 51, 71, 82, 87
discouragement 36, 52, 89
disguised inner torment 12
disillusioned 35
disorientated 27, 28, 48, 73, 93
doctor-shoppers 19
doormat mentality 17
dread 13
drifter 88
drug abuse, effects of 13, 28
easily, unduly, influenced by others
 16, 81
endurance is tested 61, 62, 75
envy 41, 42
escapism 12, 27, 28
exhaustion 15, 16, 46, 48, 59, 60, 61,
 62, 76, 85, 86
exploited by others 18, 55
failure to learn from mistakes 17, 23, 24
fanatic 70, 78
fear 5, 11-14, 21, 22, 25, 32, 42, 45, 55,
 56, 65, 66, 67, 82, 93
fear of failure 51, 52, 72

Index

fluid retention 92
focused on the worst that may happen 65
food intolerances 16, 23, 81
glaucoma 37
goal-oriented 47, 48
guilt 63, 64
hatred 41, 42
hayfever 16, 81
head cold 44
headaches 32, 48, 70, 86, 92
heart problems 78, 80, 83
hiding real feelings 11
high standards, unrealistic 31
homesickness 44
hormone imbalance 72
hypochondriacs 39, 40
hysterical 14, 55, 67, 93
immune system depletion 16, 20, 35, 37, 42, 87
impatience 16, 47, 48, 62, 84
inability to relax 48, 70, 78
indecisiveness 72
inflammatory conditions 63
insomnia 12, 48, 62, 86
insularity and detachment 83
intolerance 15, 16, 47, 70, 78
irritability 16, 30, 47
jealousy 42
jet lag 28, 61, 93
judgemental 15, 16
kidney problems 14, 56, 67
loner 84

loss of a loved one 35, 81, 82
low blood pressure 90
manipulative behaviour 25, 26
martyr 69, 70, 78
mental arguments 85
mental fatigue 45, 86
mid-life crisis 81, 88
migraine 86, 92
Monday morning feeling all day 45
mood-swings 57, 72
motivation, lack of 23, 27, 89, 90
nasal discharge 44
neediness 39
negativity 41, 92
negativity of others, protection against 42
nightmares 13, 14, 68
nostalgia 44
outside influences, vulnerable to 5, 81
over attachment 82
over-committed 31
over-dutiful 64
over-protective parent 66
over reactive 16, 65
over-sympathetic 66
oversensitive 5, 14, 16, 56, 81, 82
overstimulated 14, 22
over tired 45, 48, 62
overwhelmed 9, 31, 32
panic 67, 74, 93
past, inability to let go of 43, 63
perfectionist 16, 63, 64, 70

Index

post-nasal drip 44
procrastination 28, 46
prude 30
psychic sponge 14
psycho-somatic illness 90
regression therapies 44, 74
regret about past failure 63
rehabilitation 45, 62
reluctant psychic 14
repression of sadness 11
rescuer 33
resentment 92
resignation 89
revenge, desire for 41
rheumatic complaints 59, 63
rigidity of personality 80
Selective Sensitivity Response 6, 93
self-doubt 19, 20, 51
self-obsessed 29, 39, 40
self-reproach 63, 64
sense of 'missing out' 25, 26, 91
shame 29, 30
shock 28, 73, 74, 93
sibling rivalry 25, 26
silent sufferer 60
sinus problems 44, 86
skin reactions 16, 29, 86
sore throats, recurring 20, 26, 52
space cadet 34
speech problems 52
stomach problems 22, 56, 74, 86
stress, effects of 45, 61, 73, 74, 75
stuttering 52
sulking 26
suspicion 41
tension 22, 48, 56, 70, 71, 72, 78, 80, 86, 92
terror 14, 67, 68, 74
textbook lifestyle 69
throat complaints 20, 26, 52
thyroid dysfunction 52, 72
tonsillitis 52
trauma 62, 73, 74, 76, 93
twilight of life 38
unapproachable 83
"unclean" feeling 29, 30
ungrounded 28, 44, 73, 78, 89
unwanted thoughts 85, 86
uses others 79
vagueness 28, 89
victim mentality 91
violation, physical or emotional 74, 93
vision problems 37, 48, 86
will to dominate 79
withdrawn 12, 89
workaholic 45, 47, 70
worry 11, 12, 85, 86
yes-person 17, 18

www.ingramcontent.com/pod-product-compliance
Lightning Source LLC
Chambersburg PA
CBHW070309010526
44107CB00056B/2543